Driving With Care: Alcohol, Other Drugs, and Impaired Driving Offender Treatment-Strategies for Responsible Living

DEDICATED TO:

Our families and friends and to the clients who complete this program.

Driving With Care: Alcohol, Other Drugs, and Impaired Driving Offender Treatment-Strategies for Responsible Living

The Participant's Workbook, Level II Therapy

Kenneth W. Wanberg
Harvey B. Milkman
David S. Timken

Los Angeles | London | New Delhi
Singapore | Washington DC | Melbourne

Preparation and development of the *Driving With CARE Level I Education, Level II Education,* and *Level II Therapy Workbooks* and the *Provider's Guide* were supported by the Colorado Alcohol and Drug Abuse Division through the Persistent Drunk Driver Cash Fund under contract number OE IHM NC 000000010, $10,000; OE IHM NC 010000010, $15,000; OE IHM NC 010000013, $25,000.

The copyright holders grant, and the State of Colorado, Alcohol and Drug Abuse Division, reserves the rights to reproduce, publish, translate or otherwise use within the State of Colorado all or any of the copyrighted material contained in this publication.

Opinions are those of the authors or cited sources and do not necessarily reflect those of the Colorado Department of Human Services, Alcohol and Drug Abuse Division, State of Colorado.

For information:

 Sage Publications, Inc.
2455 Teller Road
Thousand Oaks, California 91320
E-mail: order@sagepub.com

Sage Publications Ltd.
1 Oliver's Yard
55 City Road
London EC1Y 1SP
United Kingdom

Sage Publications India Pvt. Ltd.
B-42 Panchsheel Enclave
Post Box 4109
New Delhi 110017
India

Driving With Care: Alcohol, Other Drugs, and Impaired Driving Offender Treatment
The Participant's Workbook, Level II Therapy

ISBN 1-4129-0597-4

Direct correspondence should be sent to:
The Center for Interdisciplinary Studies
899 Logan Street, Suite 207
Denver, CO 80203

04 05 06 07 10 9 8 7 6 5 4 3 2 1

Kenneth W. Wanberg, Th.D., Ph.D., is a private practice psychologist and the Director of the Center for Addictions Research and Evaluation (CARE), Arvada, CO. Harvey Milkman, Ph.D., is Professor of Psychology at The Metropolitan State College of Denver and Director of the Center for Interdisciplinary Studies, Denver, CO. David S. Timken, Ph.D., is a consultant to the Colorado Alcohol and Drug Abuse Division and Director of Timken and Associates, Boulder, CO.

Acquisitions Editor: Arthur Pomponio
Editorial Assistant: Veronica Novak
Graphic Design and Layout: Karyn Sader

TABLE OF CONTENTS

LIST OF FIGURES

LIST OF TABLES

LIST OF WORKSHEETS

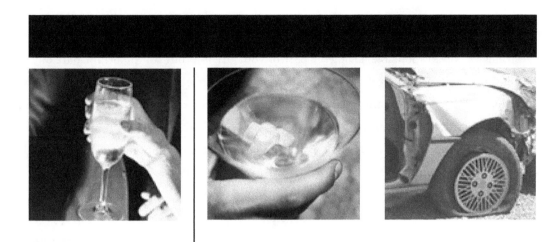

INTRODUCTION

welcome

WELCOME TO DRIVING WITH CARE: Impaired Driving Offender Treatment: Strategies for Responsible Living and Change. We will refer to this program as **Driving With Care (DWC) Therapy.** It is important that you have completed an impaired driving education program before starting this treatment program. The best preparation for DWC Therapy is to have completed **Driving With Care Level II Education.**

DWC Therapy is built on the idea that we make changes in our actions by changing how we think and by changing the attitudes and beliefs that support our thinking. Making changes in your life will help you to achieve the two main goals of **Driving with Care (DWC) Therapy:** to help you prevent future impaired driving - to prevent recidivism; and to avoid a pattern of AOD use that has caused you problems and led you to impaired driving - to prevent relapse.

We are looking at CARE as not only being an important part of your driving, but an important part of your life - caring about yourself and caring about others. Caring means being responsible to yourself, to others and to your community. What this program is really about is helping you to develop approaches and strategies for responsible living and change.

So, once again, WELCOME TO **DWC Therapy.** We invite you to take an active part in this program. As is true with most of our efforts in life, what you get out of this program will depend on the positive effort that you put into the program. We want you to have a rewarding and successful experience. We will do everything we can to make this happen.

THE PARTICIPANT'S WORKBOOK

THIS *PARTICIPANT'S WORKBOOK* provides a guide for your participation in **DWC Therapy.** For each therapy session, objectives are outlined, the key ideas are presented, and exercises and work sheets are provided that help you apply the topics and material to your own situation. We want you to take an active part in each session through sharing what you learned in the exercises and work sheets. We would like you to read the content of each session before group and complete the classroom work sheets in group. It is important that you bring your **Participant's Workbook** to each treatment session.

WHO IS THIS PROGRAM FOR?

IMPAIRED DRIVING OFFENDERS with a greater degree of alcohol or other drug (AOD) related problems and/or a repeated history of impaired driving are at higher risk for returning to a pattern of impaired driving. For these impaired driving offenders, more than just an education program is needed. **DWC Therapy** is a treatment program designed to go beyond impaired driving education to bringing about changes in attitudes, beliefs and behaviors that lead to AOD use problems and impaired driving behavior.

You are in **DWC Therapy** because your impaired driving evaluation showed a history of AOD misuse and problems and you had a high arrest BAC level (for example, .15 or higher). You may have also had prior DWI convictions, prior AOD education and treatment and other life-situation problems related to AOD use. The fact that you are in **DWC Therapy** means that you have identified or your impaired driving evaluation identified that AOD use has caused you problems in your life and that you may also have other life adjustment issues that need to be addressed.

DRIVING WHILE IMPAIRED - DWI

We will use the term DWI (Driving While Impaired) to refer to Driving While Ability Impaired (DWAI) and Driving Under the Influence (DUI). Your actual charge and/or conviction may have been a DWAI or DUI. In Colorado, DWAI is a lesser charge based on a lower Blood Alcohol Concentration (BAC) and DUI refers to a more serious charge based on a higher BAC. Other states may use another term, such as Operating While Impaired (OWI).

HOW IS DWC THERAPY STRUCTURED?

DWC Therapy has four treatment tracks. These tracks make it possible for impaired driving offenders to meet different treatment requirements placed on them by the court and/or the motor vehicle department. It provides for a basic 21 session treatment program and then a plan for extended therapy sessions.

Your specific education and treatment requirements will depend on the state or jurisdiction in which you received your DWI offense. Thus, those requirements may vary some from the DWC structure. For example, you may be required to take only 20 therapy sessions. Thus, you could meet this requirement by attending 20 of the 21 Track A DWC basic therapy sessions. Or, if you are required to take 25 treatment sessions, you would fall into **DWC Therapy** Track B, and complete the 21 basic therapy program plus four additional Track B therapy sessions.

Most DWI offenders are required to take an impaired driving education program before entering treatment or therapy. Thus, your total DWI legal requirements would include both education and treatment. For example, in Colorado, offenders in Track A of DWI treatment must take 24 hours of DWI education followed by 21 two-hour sessions of therapy.

Track A is the core or main treatment program with 21 two-hour, curriculum-based therapy sessions. Each session will have about 90 minutes of manual-guided therapy activities followed by around 30 minutes of process group focusing on the session topic and client concerns. **Sessions 1 and 2 of this program are the orientation sessions to DWC Therapy. You will complete these two sessions, by meeting individually with your counselor or in an orientation group, before continuing with sessions 3 though 21.**

Track B includes the 21 two-hour *Track A* core therapy program and an additional five two-hour *DWC Therapy* sessions. During these five sessions, clients will select two manual-guided *Therapy Projects* to work on and present in a group. There are 10 manual-guided *Therapy Projects* in this *Participant's Workbook* from which clients may select their two therapy projects. Clients will be given from 15 to 20 minutes to present their project. Clients may select a topic other than the 10 provided, if they decide there is another important area that they need to work on.

Track C includes the 21 two-hour *Track A* core therapy sessions plus 13 two-hour therapy sessions. *Track C* clients are expected to select and present at least four manual-guided therapy projects during the 13 sessions.

Track D includes the 21 two-hour *Track A* core therapy program plus 22 two-hour therapy sessions. *Track D* clients are expected to select and present eight manual-guided *Therapy Projects* during their 22 group sessions.

Track B through D clients may meet their therapy hours in several ways.
- Be assigned to a specific group for *Track B* through *D* clients.
- Individual, relationship, marital or family counseling.
- Attending *Track A* core therapy sessions as a peer-support client.
- Attend a relapse prevention or continuing care therapy group.
- Other special counseling or therapy sessions such as anger management, a therapist-led 12-Step Group.

Track B through D clients will present their therapy projects in a group that they attend.

You and your counselor will develop an individual treatment plan (ITP) based on the Master Assessment Plan (MAP) you do in Session 2. This plan will help meet any special needs you might have.

The amount of treatment to which clients are assigned usually depends on their BAC level at arrest, whether they-have had prior driving under the influence or driving while impaired (DWI) convictions, the extent of their past involvement in alcohol or other drug (AOD) use problems and other problem situations in their lives for which the evaluator felt **DWC Therapy** would be of help. Use Table 1 below to describe your specific education and treatment requirements. Write in your BAC arrest, number of prior DWI arrests, your length of education and treatment, and combined length of education and treatment.

TABLE 1			Your DWI Education and Treatment Requirements		
ARREST BAC	NUMBER PRIOR DWIS	CHECK PAST AOD PROBLEMS	LENGTH OF EDUCATION	LENGTH OF TREATMENT	COMBINED EDUCATION/ TREATMENT
		❏ Low ❏ Mediium ❏ High	Hours: Sessions: Weeks:	Hours: Sessions: Weeks:	Hours: Sessions: Weeks:

GOALS AND OBJECTIVES OF DWC THERAPY

DWC EDUCATION challenged you to look beyond the fact that you had one major AOD use problem in your life: being charged with and convicted of DWI. It gave you the tools and challenged you to take an honest look at how you might fit various kinds of AOD use and misuse patterns. **DWC Therapy** goes beyond only giving you information about AOD use and misuse and about recidivism and relapse. **DWC Therapy** is about taking action to change your thinking and behaviors not only to prevent recidivism and relapse, but to have a more positive relationship with yourself, with others and with your community. **DWC Therapy** is about learning strategies and skills to live a more responsible and meaningful life.

The picture below describes the three goals of DWC Therapy.

▶ Learn the pathways to relapse and recidivism.
▶ Learn and practice the skills to prevent future problems related to alcohol or other drug (AOD) use - prevent relapse.
▶ Learn and practice the skills to prevent future impaired driving - prevent recidivism.

These goals are met through learning three sets of skills.

▶ Cognitive or mental self-control skills.
▶ Social and relationship skills.
▶ Community responsibility skills.

These goals and skills rest on the DWC Therapy principle or concept that self-control and self-management lead to positive outcomes and responsible living and change.

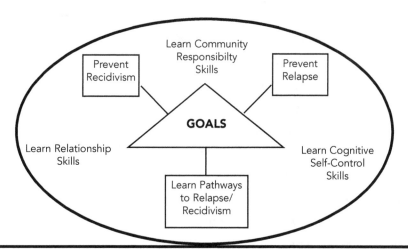

SELF-CONTROL AND SELF-MANAGEMENT
Positive Outcomes and Responsible Living and Change

Here are the specific objectives of **DWC Therapy.** These will provide you with some idea of what we want you to get out of this program.

- **Prevent recidivism:** To help you make the changes in your life to prevent recidivism and to challenge you to accept the zero tolerance-zero risk goal as the basis of your recidivism prevention plan.
- **Prevent relapse:** To help you make the changes in your life to prevent returning to a pattern of thinking and to a pattern of alcohol and other drug use that are harmful and disruptive to normal living.
- Do further work on your recidivism and relapse prevention plans using the life-style balance model.
- Apply the cognitive behavioral approach to changing thinking, beliefs and attitudes that control actions and behavior and which lead to more responsible living and change.
- Identify the patterns of and pathways to AOD addiction, abuse and dependence and to help you make changes to prevent involvement in AOD patterns of addiction, abuse and dependence.
- Help you build, strengthen and apply cognitive self-control skills to manage and change thoughts, emotions and beliefs in order to prevent negative outcomes including recidivism and relapse.
- Help you build, strengthen and apply interpersonal and social skills so as to increase positive relationship outcomes and prevent negative relationship outcomes that lead to recidivism and relapse.
- Help you build, strengthen and apply attitudes and skills to increase responsible social behavior and prevent negative relationships with the community such as DWI behavior and AOD abuse.
- Help you develop and put to work a plan for responsible living and change that will lead to positive outcomes for yourself, for others and for your community.

OUR EXPECTATIONS OF EACH OTHER: PROGRAM AGREEMENTS AND GUIDELINES

Here are the expectations and guidelines for clients in this program.

- To attend and be on time for each class and take an active part in discussing the material.
- To be respectful and have a positive attitude towards group members and program leaders.
- To keep the names of and information about members of the group in confidence and not to talk about what is learned about group members with anyone outside of the group.
- To make up any lessons that are missed.
- To complete classroom work sheets and homework.
- To not use alcohol or any mind-altering drugs while in the program and to not attend any session after using alcohol or any other drug unless prescribed by a doctor.

- To talk to the group and/or counselor about a desire to drink alcohol or use other drugs.

- To take part in any alcohol or other drug testing that is required by this agency or the court.

- To not operate a motor vehicle while impaired by alcohol or other drugs.

- To not drive a motor vehicle without a valid driver's license.

- To understand that a client has the choice to withdraw from this program at any time, yet to know that such withdrawal will be reported to the probation department or referring agency and that there may be judicial consequences for such withdrawal.

- That clients are asked to sign a consent for involvement in this program and that this consent may include the above agreements and guidelines.

WHAT ARE YOUR EXPECTATIONS OF THIS PROGRAM?

- What would you like to get from this program? What would you add to the program objectives outlined above? Share these with the group.

- What would you like to add to the above agreements so that you feel relaxed and safe and so that you can get the most out of this program? Share these with the group.

WHAT IS OUR APPROACH?

WE HAVE LISTED some very specific objectives of this program and what we would like from you. But what is our approach? What is our goal for you? How will your program counselors guide you in this program?

We will use the example of the person who is building and wanting to maintain athletic skills at a top level of performance. The first step to being a good athlete is to learn the basic skills and lessons used playing the sport. That requires practice and a willingness to commit to that sport. Then, once the basic skills and lessons of the sport are learned, there is the process of fine-tuning those skills, to maintain those skills and to stay in shape. This involves practice and getting feedback from others. Finally, we know that a good athlete CARES about his sport.

In **DWC (Driving with CARE) Education,** you learned the basic lessons and skills of preventing recidivism and relapse. You were challenged to practice those skills and even received feedback on how you were doing. We hope that you began to CARE about being responsible in preventing recidivism and relapse.

DWC Therapy helps you to fine-tune these basic lessons and skills of being a good "athlete" in responsible living. But it goes beyond these basic skills to teach you some new approaches in performing responsible living and making changes in your life. A good athlete commits to practicing the skills of his or her sport each day. Being a responsible and reliable person means that you commit yourself to practicing the skills of responsible living each day.

Most people arrested for DWI or who develop habits of unhealthy use of alcohol or who use illegal drugs may not have learned important lessons and skills that:

▶ give them self-control over their thinking and actions
▶ help them be effective in relating to others and to deal with relationship conflicts; and
▶ help them to develop and maintain responsible (trustworthy) and caring thoughts and attitudes towards the community and society.

DWC Therapy will take you down the path of doing just this – practicing the old lessons and skills and learning new lessons and skills to give you more self-control, to be even stronger in relating to others and to be more caring in your relationship to your community.

You have been told that experience is a good teacher. But experience is really not a good teacher. Yes, we learn from experience and it is important as we practice the skills that give us self-control and help us live in a responsible and caring way. But experience is often a poor teacher because many times it gives you the test before the lesson. A good teacher first gives you the lesson – so you can pass the test. Too often, we did not have the lessons to pass the life-tests we have faced.

Thus, the counselors, teachers and coaches in **DWC Therapy** will do two things:

▶ Help you become a better "athlete" in the art of living and driving by strengthening your skills, learning new ones and staying in shape; and
▶ Help you strengthen the lessons you have learned and to learn higher level skills and lessons that you may have not yet learned in order to improve and change your life and live in a more responsible manner.

This program is built on the cognitive-behavioral approach that we make changes in our actions by changing how we think, what we believe about ourselves and the world and how we feel. Change and improvement begins first in our minds. We can put it in a simple way. It is your thoughts and your beliefs and your attitudes - not what happens around you or to you - that cause you to feel and act in a certain way or cause you to do certain things. It was your *thinking* - not the events outside of yourself - that led you to a DWI arresst. In the first session of this program, we will review and revisit the cognitive-behavioral approach to learning and change.

DWC Therapy will take a deeper look at the patterns of and pathways to AOD addiction and the problems related to AOD use. We will learn skills to increase mental self-control over feelings and emotions and behavior outcomes. We will learn skills and increase knowledge that will help us to have better and more meaningful relationships with others. We will learn how to be more responsible to others and to our community.

S E S S I O N 1

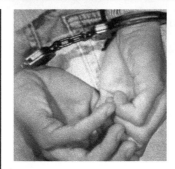

PROGRAM ORIENTATION I

UNDERSTANDING AND

ENGAGING CHANGE

OVERVIEW AND SESSION OBJECTIVES

THE FIRST PART OF THIS session will introduce you to **DWC Therapy.** This will give you an idea of how the program is set up, the overall goals and objectives of the program, our expectations of you and your participation agreements, and a summary of what approach we are taking in the learning and change process.

The second part of this session will focus on the ideas and concepts of how our thinking, attitudes and beliefs control our actions, and how we change those thoughts, beliefs and actions. We will study the six rules of thinking that lead to our actions and the three rules of learning that determine how our behaviors are strengthened. We will study the map that shows how our thinking leads to good or bad outcomes and how those outcome behaviors get strengthened or reinforced. We will look at the steps and tools for changing our thoughts and our behaviors.

OBJECTIVES OF THIS SESSION

▶ Review the introduction material to **DWC Therapy.**

▶ Review the ideas of how our thoughts, attitudes and beliefs lead to feelings and how we act.

▶ Review how our behaviors get strengthened or weakened.

▶ Practice applying the cognitive change map to how our thinking leads to good or bad outcomes and how our thoughts and behaviors get strengthened.

▶ Apply the steps and tools to changing our thoughts and behaviors.

SESSION CONTENT

WE WILL START BY LOOKING at the key ideas about changing our thoughts, beliefs, and actions. This will be a review for those who have gone through *Driving with CARE: Level I or Level II Education.*

A. WHAT IS OUR APPROACH IN DWC THERAPY?

We use a cognitive-behavioral approach to learning and change. This means that we make changes in our actions by changing how we think, what we believe about ourselves and the world and how we feel. It is your thoughts and your beliefs and your attitudes - not what happens around you or to you - that cause you to feel and act in a certain way. It was your *thinking* - not the events outside of yourself - that led you to getting a DWI. You will learn to change your mental world so as to give you more control over your life.

Here are three skills that will give you self-control in relationship to yourself, to others and your community:

▶ mental restructuring or thought changing;

▶ social and relationship skills training;

▶ community responsibility skills or skills that help you to increase reliable and responsible actions in the community.

You may be thinking, "I don't have to change or even improve myself." The fact is that your patterns of thinking and living led you to driving under the influence of alcohol or other drugs and brought you here.

Self-control leads to positive outcomes. Self-control comes from managing our thoughts and being responsible in our relationships with others and our community.

B. SIX RULES OF THINKING THAT LEAD TO ACTIONS OR BEHAVIORS

1. **Thinking Rule One:** Your thoughts, attitudes and beliefs -not what happens outside of you - control your emotions, your actions and your behaviors.

   ▶ **Automatic thoughts:** a thinking pattern or thought habit already formed inside our heads. We call them thought habits.

   ▶ An **attitude** is a thought for or against a situation, person, idea or object outside of ourselves. It directs how we think, feel and act. It is usually hooked into an emotion or feeling. It is usually described in terms of being "good" or "bad," "positive" or "negative."

   ▶ A **belief** is a value or idea that we use to judge or evaluate outside events, situations, people or ourselves. A belief bonds you to the outside event. It is more powerful than an attitude, but will direct your attitudes towards things or people. We all have a set of *core beliefs*. Share in group what you see as some core beliefs that led to your DWI behavior.

   Exercise: Use *Work Sheet 1,* page 20, to identify some of your automatic thoughts, attitudes and beliefs that led to your DWI behavior.

2. **Thinking Rule Two:** We often resist or fight changing our thinking, attitudes and beliefs. When we do this, we defend our view of ourselves. Remember when you were arrested for DWI? Was your first thought "I only had a few drinks, I wasn't really drunk?" Do you still believe that? If not, then you have changed your thinking and beliefs.

   ▶ What are some ways you are still fighting change in your drinking or other drug use?

◗ We fight changing some of our beliefs. We call this the *Belief Clutch*. It is a do or die view of ourselves. What are some belief clutches you have around drinking or other drug use? Remember the story about the Flying Walendas? The father taught each member of the troupe to always hold on to the balancing pole, no matter what. When a gust of wind caught him off balance, his thought was "hold on to the pole." He fell 12 stories to his death. His hands were so tightly "clutched" to the pole they had to be pried loose. Had he let go of the pole and grabbed the wire, he might have lived. Are you still clutching?

3. **Thinking Rule Three:** We make choices about the thoughts we have about ourselves and about the outside world. This means you can be in control of your thoughts. What are some choices you make that lead to bad outcomes? What are some that lead to good outcomes?

4. **Thinking Rule Four:** There can be errors in our thinking or thought habits (automatic thoughts) about the outside world and about ourselves. These are *errors in logic* that can lead to bad outcomes. Here are some: "blaming others," "don't care," "don't need help," "stubborn-thinking-won't change," "lying," and "better than others." What are some thinking errors that you still use that lead to bad outcomes?

5. **Thinking Rule Five:** Before you act, train yourself to think, "What is best for me in the long term?" "What is in my best interest?" Take the *long-term look*. It will help you think about the results or outcome of your actions. Would thinking this way have stopped you from driving impaired?

6. **Thinking Rule Six:** What happens outside of you **will** bring on certain thoughts based on your beliefs and attitudes. We call these *events*. But remember, you choose what you think about and how you react to those events.

C. THREE RULES OF LEARNING THAT STRENGTHEN OR REINFORCE OUR BEHAVIORS OR ACTIONS

When our thoughts and beliefs lead to an action or behavior, the thoughts leading to the action get reinforced **and** the behavior also gets reinforced. The behavior repeats itself. **The thoughts and behavior are learned.** The behavior may form a behavior habit or action habit. Now we have **thought habits** or automatic thoughts and **action habits** or automatic behaviors. *How does this learning of action habits take place?*

1. **Learning Rule I:** If a behavior turns on something positive such as a pleasant feeling or a sense of well-being, that behavior gets strethened and most likely repeats itself. It may become a habit. This is the *turning on positive events rule*. If drinking alcohol makes us feel good, gives us pleasure or turns on positive feelings, then drinking is reinforced. We will do it again to feel good.

2. **Learning Rule II:** If a behavior turns off a negative event - something that is unpleasant, stressful or painful - that behavior gets strengthened and will be learned. It will become a behavior habit. We call this *Turning Off Negative Events Rule*. This is the most powerful way to reinforce behavior. When we feel stressed, we take a drink, the stress goes away. This reinforces the drinking.

3. **Learning Rule III:** If a behavior turns on a negative event - something unpleasant, stress or depression - that behavior should be weakened, or never occur again. We will call this the *Turning on Negative Events Rule.* We drink too much. We get sick, have a bad hangover. This rule says we should not drink like that again.

However, *Learning Rule III* doesn't always work. Why do we continue behaviors which cause us problems? Why would you ever drink to excess again if you got sick from drinking? **Here are some reasons.**

▶ First, it's the power of *Rules I and II.* Behaviors that turn on something pleasant or turn off something unpleasant give us immediate rewards even though those behaviors can lead to negative or bad outcomes or pain.

▶ Second, it is the power of the thoughts that lead to the outcome. *Learning Rule III* doesn't always work because the bad results from a behavior also strengthen our automatic thoughts and beliefs that led to the behavior and bad outcome.

▶ Third, *Learning Rule III* doesn't always work because thoughts and behaviors *do not always* lead to a bad outcome. We have too much to drink, we drive and get by with it. Our behavior is not punished because we don't get caught, and our thoughts that led us to the driving, **"I can get by with it,"** get reinforced or strengthened.

D. THE MAP FOR COGNITIVE-BEHAVIORAL LEARNING AND CHANGE MAP

Figure 1, page 14 gives the map that shows **how thoughts lead to feelings and actions and how those thoughts get strengthened and reinforced.** *This is illustrated by the lines that return from positive outcomes to our automatic thoughts or the lines from the negative or bad outcomes that return to our automatic thoughts.*

When we experience an outside event or a memory inside of ourselves we usually respond with an automatic thought.

▶ The automatic thought could be an **expectation** - what we expect if we do a certain thing. "If I take a drink, I'll relax."

▶ It could be an **appraisal** - thoughts that judge or give meaning to what happens to us and what we do. "I can drive. I've only had a few beers."

▶ **Attribution** - why we think things happen to us or explanations of certain outcomes. "I got this DUI because the cops were after me."

▶ **Decision** - thoughts about what we decide to do. "I'll drive home. I won't get caught."

These automatic thoughts could be *errors in thinking.* Errors in thinking often lead to bad outcomes.

Figure 1 shows that there are core attitudes, values and beliefs within us that lead to our automatic thoughts. To make lasting changes in ourselves, we must change our core beliefs and attitudes.

Figure 1 also shows that our behaviors are strengthened when the outcomes of our actions are positive. This is the arrow that goes from the positive outcome back to the positive action. The action or behavior can be any response such as drinking or talking to a friend. It is the result of the behavior that counts.

Note, there is no arrow going from the bad or negative outcomes back to the negative or maladaptive action or behavior. Avoiding the maladaptive or negative behavior may become an action habit. But regardless of the outcome of the behavior - positive (adaptive) or negative (maladaptive), good or bad - the automatic thoughts are most often strengthened. The thought habits, the beliefs, the feelings, the attitudes are strengthened. They are reinforced - learned. They become stronger **thought habits** - automatic thoughts. **EVEN BAD OUTCOMES STRENGTHEN THE THOUGHTS THAT LEAD TO THEM.**

E. USING THE COGNITIVE-BEHAVIORAL (CB) MAP TO MAKE CHANGES

How can we make changes? By *changing our thinking* so that we take positive adaptive action that leads to a good outcome. **Good outcomes will strengthen the thoughts that lead to them.** This is shown by the arrowed line going from good outcomes to our automatic thoughts. But good outcomes also strengthen the behaviors that lead to them. This is the arrow that goes from positive outcomes to adaptive actions.

▶ We will use the cognitive-behavorial (CB) Map every session to see how we handle events and how to change our thoughts, attitudes and beliefs in order to have better outcomes.
▶ We will call this the **CB Map Exercise.**

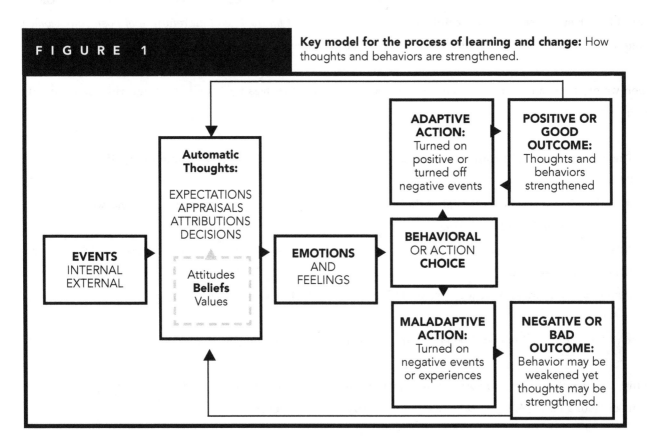

FIGURE 1

Key model for the process of learning and change: How thoughts and behaviors are strengthened.

F.   MENTAL/COGNITIVE SKILLS TO CHANGE OUR THINKING AND OUR ACTIONS

▶ **Self-Talk.** Teaching ourselves by talking to ourselves. Here are some self-talk methods.

- **Thought Stopping:** I want to stop being distrustful. If I think, "I can't trust this person," I can stop this automatic thinking by saying, "I'm feeling distrustful, I'm not going to think this way." You may still feel slightly distrustful, but you interrupted your automatic thinking and made yourself think new thoughts.

- **Thinking "Responsibility" and "Their Position:"** What if I were in THEIR POSITION? What are they thinking? RESPECT the other person as a human being. Think of THE PERSON YOU WANT TO BE. "Responsibility" and "Their Position" help us to think and act in a prosocial way. They help us take responsibility for our own behavior and place ourselves in the other person's position.

- **Planting a Positive Thought:** When you find yourself into negative thinking, *replace a negative thought with a positive thought.* Do it every time it happens. Negative thoughts will lead to negative behavior. When you change your negative thinking or thought-habits, you will have different and more positive thoughts toward people with whom you normally have problems.

- **Countering or Going Against a Thought:** Arguing against an error in thinking or a thought that does not make sense makes that thought weaker. A counter can be one statement: "That's stupid." "Not true." Sometimes it is a coping statement: "I can do it." Or a self-supporting statement: "I'm not perfect." Babe Ruth hit 714 home runs but struck out 1,330 times!

▶ **Get an image:** Imagine yourself doing a new behavior that can follow your new thought. Is it a better outcome? Imagine yourself talking slower, being calm.

▶ **Shifting the View — Perceptual Shifting:**   This is *changing our mental sets or views.* Getting caught up in destructive and damaging beliefs and thoughts can lead to AOD misuse and even DWI conduct. These often are errors of how we think about the world. If we can change our view, we can see the other side of the belief or thought. The brain can shift what it sees.

Over a long period of time, you may have held on to the belief "I deserve more than what I'm getting. I've been cheated." This view of yourself and the world can lead to going out and getting what you feel you have coming. It may lead to you doing something irresponsible. It may lead to failing to *Drive With CARE.*

▶ **Exaggerate or Overstate the Thought:** When Victor Frankl, a famous psychiatrist, was in a German concentration camp, he found people wanting to give up. He would say "Go ahead and give up. See if I care. Do it right now. Give up." He found that often this forced the person back to reality and doing just the opposite. When you find yourself worrying about something in an irrational way (a way that doesn't make sense), you can say, "OK, I'm going to worry about this for the next ten hours. I'll show you how much I can worry about this." This forces us to look at the error in our thinking.

▶ **Conditioning - Making our thoughts weaker or stronger:** Reward the positive thoughts. Make your destructive or negative thoughts weaker. If you think about driving after you have had several drinks, then think about all of the bad things that happened because of your DWI arrest. When you replace drinking with a positive activity, think about the rewards that come from the positive activity. When you want to drink but do not, reward yourself. Buy yourself something.

▶ **Logical (sensible) Study - going to court with your thought:** Fighting your nonsense (irrational) thoughts with logic or (sensible) thinking. You want to go get drunk. **Think:** Does this make sense? In the long run, is it logical? Three simple steps to this technique:

- state your thought;
- get your evidence;
- make your verdict - is it sensible or an error in thinking?

This gives you time to think it through!

▶ **Relaxation Skills:** When under stress, tense, or tired, we let our automatic thoughts or thought habits and behavior habits take over. The fatigue and stress reduce our mental control. Learning to relax gives us control. Here are some relaxation skills that give you self-control.

- **Muscle relaxation:** Learn to tense and then relax your muscles one at a time.
- **Imagining calm scenes:** Put yourself in a calm and relaxing place such as on the ocean side, by a mountain stream.
- **Mentally relaxing parts of your body:** By closing your eyes and saying to yourself - "my arms are heavy and relaxed; my forehead is cool, my hands are warm."
- **Deep breathing** is a powerful relaxation skill that you can do at any time. You take in your breath deeply and let it out; we do this almost naturally when we give a "sigh" of relief.

Now, start to use these techniques. Feel their power to help you change your thinking and actions.

Exercise: Each group member will be asked to use one of these skills. For example, you may be asked to state out loud a negative thought and then replace it with a positive thought.

G. HERE IS HOW THOUGHTS LEAD TO ACTIONS. FOLLOW THESE STEPS IN FIGURE 1 ABOVE, PAGE 14.

Step One: Look at an **event** that in the past led to a bad or negative outcome. It may have been an argument with someone, going to a party, or getting a DWI.

Step Two: What were your **thoughts?** "He doesn't understand me"? "I'll get drunk"?

Step Three: What was your **attitude?** Was it negative? Was it "The hell with you"?

Step Four: Try to identify the underlying **belief**. "I've never been treated fairly"?

Step Five: What did you **feel?** Were you angry? Were you sad? Were you stressed?

Step Six: What was your action or **behavior** that followed? Remember, you chose that action.

Step Seven: What was the **outcome** of your behavior? Was it a good or bad outcome?

REMEMBER, EVEN BAD OUTCOMES WILL STRENGTHEN THE THOUGHTS THAT LEAD TO THEM

H. REVIEWING THE STEPS TO CHANGING YOUR THOUGHTS AND YOUR BEHAVIORS

Step One: Recognize the thoughts that will lead to problem behaviors.

Step Two: Change your thoughts THAT LEAD TO BAD OUTCOMES. Imagine the positive outcomes that can follow the new thoughts. Repeat offenders did not change their thinking that led to their first DWI arrest.

Step Three: Get in touch with your feelings that come from your new thoughts. Do you feel more in control? Are your feelings more positive?

Step Four: Change your attitudes and beliefs. This is hard. You might have discovered that one of your beliefs is "Life has not been fair." Change that belief. "Some good things have happened to me."

Step Five: Think in the direction of behaviors and actions that will turn on positive events. and turn off negative events but do not lead to bad outcomes. Instead of going to the bar to relax and drink with friends to turn on good feelings, go to the gym and work out to feel good.

Step Six: Make a list of the behaviors that led to bad outcomes or caused problems. Make a list of behaviors that have led to good outcomes. Go back to the thoughts that led to those behaviors. What were the beliefs underneath those thought?

Step Seven: Reward your positive thinking and behaviors that turn on positive events or turn off negative events **but that lead to good outcomes.** Make a list of things that reward you. You deserve to have good outcomes. Reward those behaviors.

I. WHAT IS YOUR RECIDIVISM PREVENTION GOAL?

The most important goal of *Driving With CARE* and this treatment program is to prevent recidivism. In **Driving with CARE Education,** you defined your recidivism prevention goal. As we begin this program, we would like for you to state that goal. Here are the two recidivism prevention goals you can choose from.

▶ To prevent legal recidivism:
- to never drive a motor vehicle when your BAC is .05 or higher, or if you are under the age of 21, if your BAC is .02 or higher; and
- to never drive at any time when you are under the influence of mind-changing or behavior-changing drugs.

▶ To being alcohol and drug free every time you drive a motor vehicle - or the goal of zero tolerance-zero risk.

Recidivism is not just getting caught for impaired driving. It is any time where you drive when your BAC is outside the legal limits or when you are impaired by other drugs.

Exercise: You are asked to write your recidivism prevention goal in the space below. Is this goal different or the same as the one you wrote in **Driving with CARE Education**? Share this with the group.

YOUR RECIDIVISM PREVENTION GOAL

J. EXERCISES:

▶ Do *Work Sheet 1.* page 20, List thoughts, attitudes, and beliefs that you had when drinking and driving.
▶ Complete *Work Sheet 2*, page 21. You may have done this exercise in **Driving with CARE Education.** We are asking you to do it again.

Have the event represent what took place right before you were arrested for DWI. Write in that event in the top rectangle, such as, "Was at a party." In the second rectangle, on the right side, write what your thoughts were during the event, such as, "I've had a tough week, life is tough, things are not going well. I'm gonna get high and cut loose." Were these thoughts **expectations, attributions, appraisals** or **decisions**? Identify your attitudes, beliefs and feelings on the right side of the next rectangle. Your ACTION CHOICE was to "drive after drinking." In the NEGATIVE ACTION rectangle, there is written "drove after drinking." "Arrested for DWI" is written in the NEGATIVE OUTCOME rectangle. Did getting arrested strengthen the thoughts you had around the event, such as "life is tough, things are not going well?" Add to the ACTION CHOICE, NEGATIVE ACTION and NEGATIVE OUTCOMES rectangles.

Now, go back and change your thoughts. On the left side of the THOUGHTS rectangle, write new thoughts that are different from the ones on the right side. What thoughts can you put there that can lead to positive feelings and a positive outcome other than a DWI? What are the new feelings that come from those thoughts? Write in those feelings. What are the attitudes and beliefs that you need to have to produce those thoughts? Write in the new attitudes and beliefs. What are the action choices and positive actions that these changes lead to? Write in a behavior other than driving while impaired. Write in the positive or adaptive outcome. How does that outcome strengthen the changes you made in your thinking, in your attitudes and your beliefs? Work on this in class and share your work with the group.

If you did this in **Driving with CARE Education,** how did your work on this now differ? Were you more open? Was it easier? Discuss this in group.

SESSION OR HOMEWORK ACTIVITY

Use *Work Sheet 3,* page 22, and list the problem areas you need to work on during your **DWC Therapy** program. We will use this in our next *Orientation Session.*

CLOSURE PROCESS GROUP

Share with your group the following:

▶ your name;
▶ your best understanding of why you were referred to **Level II Therapy;**
▶ what you want to get out of the program; and
▶ your concerns and worries about being in the program.

You will also be asked to share what you did in *Work Sheets 1 and 2.*

List some automatic thoughts, attitudes and beliefs that are part of your DWI behavior. These are thoughts, attitudes and beliefs that you had when you drove and knew you had too much to drink or you knew you were impaired.

YOUR THINKING, ATTITUDES, AND BELIEFS WHEN DRIVING WHILE IMPAIRED

Automatic thought(s):

Attitude(s):

Belief(s):

NOTES

_____

_____

_____

_____

_____

_____

_____

_____

_____

_____

_____

_____

_____

_____

The process of cognitive and behavioral learning and change.
Complete this picture. Take an event that took place before your
DWI arrest. On the right side of the rectangle, note your thoughts,
your feelings attitudes and beliefs leading up to the DWI. Go back
and change your thoughts, feelings, beliefs and attitudes. Now write
in a positive action and the outcome.

WORKSHEET 2

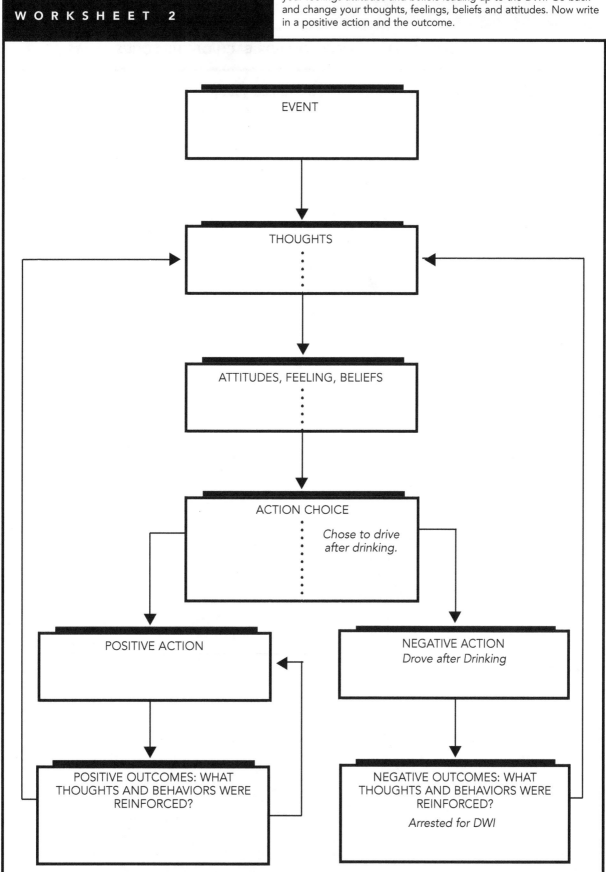

LIST PROBLEMS THAT YOU NEED TO WORK ON FOR EACH OF THE FOCUS AREAS

A. Problem areas you carried over from childhood and youth:

B. Alcohol and other drug use problems:

C. Problems related to your DWI:

D. Problem thinking, feeling and attitudes:

LIST PROBLEMS THAT YOU NEED TO WORK ON FOR EACH OF THE FOCUS AREAS

E. Current life situation problems

EMPLOYMENT AND JOB PROBLEMS:

LIVING SITUATION AND ACCOMMODATIONS:

SOCIAL AND RELATIONSHIP PROBLEMS:

MARITAL AND FAMILY ISSUES AND PROBLEMS:

EMOTIONAL-PSYCHOLOGICAL PROBLEM AREAS:

PHYSICAL HEALTH PROBLEMS:

PROBLEMS WITH THE LAW:

S E S S I O N   2

PROGRAM ORIENTATION II

TARGETS AND TOOLS FOR CHANGE

The Master Skills, your Master Profile

and your Master Assessment Plan

OVERVIEW AND SESSION OBJECTIVES

Self-awareness is a key to opening the door to change our thinking, feelings and actions. There are two pathways to self-awareness. One is through *self-disclosure* - sharing and disclosing our personal experiences and problems. The other is to receive *feedback* - having others tell us what they see and feel about what we have shared.

Self-disclosure is not easy. During much of our lives, we have been told to not talk about our feelings and problems. If we did express our feelings and thoughts, we often were put down or even punished for what we said. Often we were told not to get angry or to be happy when we were sad. If we did show our feelings, it was after we stored them up and then they came out by blowing up or throwing a tantrum or pouting.

During our childhood or teen years, we most likely were not taught ways to tell our thoughts or show our feelings in healthy ways. We were often taught to blame others, since that is the way most adults solve their frustrations and problems. We learned to solve problems by someone being right and someone being wrong. An important part of this program is talking about yourself. We want you to express your feelings and thoughts, explore your past and present feelings, explore your thoughts and actions and to tell us your story.

Receiving **feedback** is also difficult. Often, what we get from people is not feedback, but a **reaction** to what we have said or done. It is often a judgment of us, telling us we are wrong or blaming us. Feedback is most helpful when people make it clear that this is how they see us, their opinion. We listen to feedback when people relate to us and not just react to what we say or do. We listen to feedback when we feel the *other person understands us*. When this happens, we learn about ourselves. We become more aware of who and what we are. During this program, you will get feedback from your counselor and from your peers. But the feedback will be given to you in a non-blaming manner.

This session looks at the tools and targets for strengthening responsible living, self-management and making changes in our lives. We do an in-depth assessment of our life-issues and problems. We then build a master plan and look at tools that guide our efforts for self-improvement and change.

OBJECTIVES OF THIS SESSION

- Preview the Master Skills for responsible living and change.
- Complete the Master Profile - your self-disclosure.
- Your provider will do a Master Profile on you. This is feedback from your provider.
- From the Master Profile, identify or define targets of change and complete your Master Assessment Plan (MAP).
- Learn how to do a thinking report.
- Learn how to do an autobiography.
- Begin our weekly AOD monitoring chart.

SESSION CONTENT AND FOCUS

SELF-DISCLOSURE IS NECESSARY for self-awareness and self-awareness leads to self-improvement and change. The tools and skills that you review and learn in this session are directed at bringing about self-awareness and open the doors for self-improvement and change. Remember the overall goals of DWC Therapy: to prevent relapse and to prevent recidivism into impaired driving.

A. THE MASTER SKILLS: TOOLS FOR RESPONSIBLE LIVING AND CHANGE

Skill building and practice is a core part of impaired driving education and therapy. In **DWC Therapy,** we continue to learn and strengthen the use of these skills. We will call these the *Master Skills* for responsible living, self-management and change. There are three groups of skills.

▶ **Mental restructuring skills** to change and strengthen thoughts, attitudes and beliefs for positive outcomes.
▶ **Relationship responsibility skills** to change and strengthen positive relationships with others.
▶ **Society responsibility skills** to increase reliable and responsible actions in the community and society.

Table 2, page 31, gives you the Master Skills list, divided into the three categories. An importnant part of growth and change is self-evaluation. Thus, after each DWC Therapy Session, you will be asked to update the list by:

▶ writing in the date you worked on the skill;
▶ rating your level of mastery in using the skill; and
▶ reevaluate and update your level of mastery on skills you learned.

For example, one skill is using the *Cognitive Behavioral (CB) Map.* Write in the date that you first learned that skill. Then, rate your level of mastery in using the CB Map for self-management and change. You will then review your mastery of this skill from time to time. The goal is for you to reach a "Good" to "Very Good" level of mastery for all *Master Skills.*

Some of the *Master Skills* can provide self-management and change in both areas of relationship and society. For example, *preventing relapse skills* can improve responsibility towards others and towards society. *Empathy skills* can increase positive realtionships with others and responsible actions in society.

Exercise: In Session 1, you worked on the Cognitive Behavior Map skill, number 1 in Table 2, page 31. Put the date you attended Session 1 and rate your mastery level on this skill.

B. THE MASTER PROFILE TOOL FOR SELF-ASSESSMENT

When you were admitted to **Driving with CARE Therapy,** you completed tests and questionnaires to evaluate situations and conditions in your life, particularly your AOD use and misuse. You completed *Work Sheet 3* which helped you look at various problem areas in living. We will now use this information to build your *Master Profile (MP).* The areas of assessment in the MP are:

- Your patterns of AOD use and abuse;
- Impaired driving problems and risk;
- Your thinking, feeling and attitude patterns;
- Problems of childhood and youth;
- Your life situation problems and conditions, and
- Your motivation for treatment and readiness for change.

Exercise: Build your *Master Profile (MP)* by completing *Work Sheet 4,* pages 32-34. Your counselor will also complete an MP on you and you will compare that MP with yours.

C. BUILDING THE MASTER ASSESSMENT PLAN - TARGETS FOR CHANGE

Use the MP to build your *Master Assessment Plan (MAP)* which gives you a plan and targets for change. It guides your involvement in DWC Therapy. It helps you see the specific problem areas and conditions that you need to work on and change.

Exercise: Complete the MAP in *Work Sheet 5,* pages 35-38, with the help of counselor and group. You will add to and update your MAP while in **DWC Therapy.** This is your individual treatment plan.

D. TOOLS FOR DIRECTING CHANGE

There are three parts to our mental life: *memories, the here-and-now, and our dreams.* **Memories** are the basis of our history - our autobiography. Our memories come from how we choose to live each day. How we live each day and how we choose to handle what happens to us determines our future. We will use five tools to review our history, monitor what happens to us in the here-and-now, and make choices about our future.

1. Your Autobiography

You are asked to write your *autobiography* over the next six to eight weeks. The autobiography describes our roots and our past experiences. Not all of our history and our roots are pleasant. But it is important that we look at both the unpleasant and the pleasant, the negative parts as well as the positive parts of our history. This is why it is not easy to write your autobiography. But it is important in your effort to make changes in your life.

If you have already written your *autobiography,* do not do it over. Read it again. Add any parts of your history that are not included. We also want you to write about your future. You are asked to write your autobiography in a separate notebook using this outline:

- Describe the family you grew up in.
- Describe your childhood from first memories through teen years.
- Describe your adult years including your education, jobs, marriage(s) and interests.
- Then, write a history of your DWI behavior, to include when you first started impaired driving, how often and under what situations.
- Write your history of AOD use. Begin with your first use of alcohol or other drugs.
- Describe what brought you into this program.
- Now, write about your future. Dreaming, setting goals and planning are the maps of living. Put these in this part of your autobiography.

2. Your Thinking Reports.

The *Thinking Report* captures your **response to the here-and-now.** A thinking report will help you to pay attention to your thoughts, feelings, beliefs and your actions. Here are the five parts of the thinking report.

- **Event:** Describe in a few words the situation. Be factual and describe what you see (or be objective). Do not write thoughts or feelings.
- **Thoughts:** What thoughts do you remember? You do not have to explain or make excuses.
- **Feelings:** Make a list all the feelings you had: Nervous, angry, irritated.
- **Attitudes and Beliefs:** What attitudes and beliefs are related to this event?
- **Outcome:** What was your action and behavior that came out of the event?

3. Your RE-THINKING Report.

Our **re-thinking report** describes how we would change our responses to the events that we experience. It represents a guide for change and our plan on how we will handle **future** events. The re-thinking report has the same parts as the thinking report, but it changes the thoughts, the feelings, beliefs and actions from the thinking report to produce positive or good outcomes. You will be asked to do thinking and re-thinking reports either during your sessions or for homework.

4. AOD Weekly Monitoring Chart.

One of the agreements we ask you to make in **DWC Therapy** is to not use alcohol or other drugs (not prescribed by a doctor) while in the program. Yet, here is what happens to some clients while in **DWC Therapy**.

a. They think about using alcohol or other drugs - high-risk thinking.

b. They find themselves in drinking or other drug-use situations, such as the bar, with drinking friends.

c. Even though they agree not to drink or use drugs, they may "lapse" back into use or relapse back into a pattern of use.

d. During those lapses, they may find themselves thinking about driving.

e. Or, during those lapses, they may actually drive while using alcohol or other drugs.

Most clients in **DWC Therapy** will have *a* and *b* above happen to them. Some may have *c, d, or e* happen to them. We ask you to monitor the above five possibilities each week. Be as honest as you can. If *a* and *b* happen to you, use the mental-behavioral skills to change the thinking or behavior.

If c, d, or e happens to you, put that on your AOD Weekly Monitoring Chart. Then talk about it with your counselor and group. Ask them to help you. Use the cognitive-behavior skills to change the thinking or behavior. Don't let it continue. This is for your safety and the safety of others.

The Weekly Monitoring Chart is found in the back of this Participant's Workbook. There is a column for each of the five things above that can happen to you.

5. **Client Progress Report.**

One tool for change is to report to your community the progress that you are making in the DWC Therapy. One way that you meet your obligation to the community and yourself is to complete this **DWC Therapy** program. As part of fulfilling your obligation to the community, you are asked to make a report to your community through your probation officer of your progress in **DWC Therapy** by completing the *Client Progress Report (CPR)* in the back of this Participant's Workbook:

▶ at the end of your eighth session;
▶ and at the end of your 20th session.

CLOSURE

Because of the amount of material in this session, you may have only a few minutes to share with your counselor or orientation group.

	DESCRIPTION OF SKILLS	**DATE BEGAN**	**LEVEL OF SKILL MASTERY**			
			POOR	**FAIR**	**GOOD**	**VERY GOOD**
MENTAL SKILLS	1. Cognitive behavioral map					
	2. Mental restructuring skills					
	3. Relaxation skills					
	4. Changing AOD use patterns					
	5. Preventing AOD problems					
	6. Managing urges/cravings					
	7. Change negative thinking					
	8. Change thinking errors					
	9. Managing stress/anxiety					
	10. Managing depression					
RELATIONSHIP SKILLS	11. Anger management skills					
	12. Reading non-verbal cues					
	13. Active sharing skills					
	14. Active listening skills					
	15. Starting a conversation					
	16. Giving compliments/praise					
	17. Receiving compliments					
	18. Problem-solving skills					
	19. Assertiveness skills					
	20. Close relations skills					
	21. Manage high-risk exposures					
SOCIETY SKILLS	22. Refusal skills					
	23. Preventing relapse					
	24. Lifestyle balance skills					
	25. Preventing recidivism					
	26. Prosocial skills					
	27. Strengthen moral character					
	28. Empathy skills					
	29. Conflict resolution skills					
	30. Negotiation skills					

TABLE 2

Master Skills List for Self-management, Responsible Living and Change: put the date you started work on the skill and rate your mastery level. Update your level of mastery after each session. Make **Good to Very Good** your goal for each skill.

I. ALCOHOL AND OTHER DRUG USE ASSESSMENT

	LEVEL OF INVOLVEMENT IN DRUG USE		
YOUR QUANTITY/FREQUENCY OF USE	**NONE OR LOW**	**MODERATE**	**HIGH**
Alcohol Involvement	1 2 3	4 5 6 7	8 9 10
Marijuana Involvement	1 2 3	4 5 6 7	8 9 10
Cocaine Involvement	1 2 3	4 5 6 7	8 9 10
Amphetamine Involvement	1 2 3	4 5 6 7	8 9 10
Other Drugs	1 2 3	4 5 6 7	8 9 10
STYLE OF ALCOHOL/OTHER DRUG USE	**NONE OR LOW**	**MODERATE**	**HIGH**
Convivial or Gregarious Use	1 2 3	4 5 6 7	8 9 10
Solo or Use by Yourself	1 2 3	4 5 6 7	8 9 10
Sustained or Continuous Use	1 2 3	4 5 6 7	8 9 10
BENEFITS OF AOD USE TO...	**NONE OR LOW**	**MODERATE**	**HIGH**
Cope with Social Discomfort	1 2 3	4 5 6 7	8 9 10
Cope with Emotional Discomfort	1 2 3	4 5 6 7	8 9 10
Cope with Relationships	1 2 3	4 5 6 7	8 9 10
Cope with Physical Distress	1 2 3	4 5 6 7	8 9 10
NEGATIVE CONSEQUENCES OF USE	**NONE OR LOW**	**MODERATE**	**HIGH**
Behavioral Disruption from Use	1 2 3	4 5 6 7	8 9 10
Emotional Disruption from Use	1 2 3	4 5 6 7	8 9 10
Physical Disruption from Use	1 2 3	4 5 6 7	8 9 10
Social Irresponsibility from Use	1 2 3	4 5 6 7	8 9 10
Overall Negative Consequences	1 2 3	4 5 6 7	8 9 10
CATEGORIES OF AOD USE PROBLEMS	**NONE OR LOW**	**MODERATE**	**HIGH**
Drinking/Drug Use Problem	1 2 3	4 5 6 7	8 9 10
Problem Drinker or Drug Use	1 2 3	4 5 6 7	8 9 10
Alcohol/Other Drug Abuse	1 2 3	4 5 6 7	8 9 10
Alcohol/Other Drug Dependent	1 2 3	4 5 6 7	8 9 10

II. IMPAIRED DRIVING ASSESSMENT

	LEVEL OF PROBLEM SEVERITY		
AREAS OF IMPAIRED DRIVING PROBLEMS AND RISK	NONE OR LOW	MODERATE	HIGH
BAC Level at Time of Arrest	1 2 3	4 5 6 7	8 9 10
Disruption to your Lifestyle	1 2 3	4 5 6 7	8 9 10
Bodily Injury to Yourself	1 2 3	4 5 6 7	8 9 10
Bodily Injury to Others	1 2 3	4 5 6 7	8 9 10
Property Damage Including Car	1 2 3	4 5 6 7	8 9 10
Overall Problems From DWI	1 2 3	4 5 6 7	8 9 10
Overall Driving Risk	1 2 3	4 5 6 7	8 9 10

III. ASSESSMENT OF THINKING, FEELING AND ATTITUDE PATTERNS

	LEVEL OF PROBLEM SEVERITY		
THINKING, FEELINGS, TRIGGERS AND ATTITUDE PATTERNS THAT CAN LEAD TO DWI BEHAVIOR/CONDUCT	NONE OR LOW	MODERATE	HIGH
Blame Others for Problems	1 2 3	4 5 6 7	8 9 10
Victim Stance	1 2 3	4 5 6 7	8 9 10
Careless: Don't Care	1 2 3	4 5 6 7	8 9 10
Think You Are Better Than Others	1 2 3	4 5 6 7	8 9 10
Irresponsible Thinking	1 2 3	4 5 6 7	8 9 10
Act Without Thinking	1 2 3	4 5 6 7	8 9 10
Angry and Aggressive Thinking	1 2 3	4 5 6 7	8 9 10
Feeling Depressed and Sad	1 2 3	4 5 6 7	8 9 10
Rebellious Against Authority	1 2 3	4 5 6 7	8 9 10
Time with Drinking Friends	1 2 3	4 5 6 7	8 9 10
Friends Angry at Laws and Society	1 2 3	4 5 6 7	8 9 10
Conflict with Spouse/Family	1 2 3	4 5 6 7	8 9 10
Second Home at Bar	1 2 3	4 5 6 7	8 9 10
Having Bad/Unpleasant Feelings	1 2 3	4 5 6 7	8 9 10
Loss of Self-Importance	1 2 3	4 5 6 7	8 9 10
Loss of Someone Important	1 2 3	4 5 6 7	8 9 10

IV. BACKGROUND: PROBLEMS OF CHILDHOOD AND DEVELOPMENT

	LEVEL OF PROBLEM SEVERITY		
PROBLEMS IN CHILDHOOD AND TEENAGE YEARS	**NONE OR LOW**	**MODERATE**	**HIGH**
Teenage Alcohol/Drug Use	1 2 3	4 5 6 7	8 9 10
Problems with Law During Teens	1 2 3	4 5 6 7	8 9 10
Problems with Parents/Family	1 2 3	4 5 6 7	8 9 10
Emotional-Psychological	1 2 3	4 5 6 7	8 9 10
School Adjustment Problems	1 2 3	4 5 6 7	8 9 10
Physical Illness in Childhood	1 2 3	4 5 6 7	8 9 10

V. CURRENT LIFE SITUATION PROBLEMS

	LEVEL OF PROBLEM SEVERITY		
AREAS OF ADULT PROBLEMS	**NONE OR LOW**	**MODERATE**	**HIGH**
Job and Employment Problems	1 2 3	4 5 6 7	8 9 10
Financial and Money Problems	1 2 3	4 5 6 7	8 9 10
Unstable Living Situation	1 2 3	4 5 6 7	8 9 10
Social-Relationship Problems	1 2 3	4 5 6 7	8 9 10
Marital-Family Problems	1 2 3	4 5 6 7	8 9 10
Emotional-Psychological	1 2 3	4 5 6 7	8 9 10
Problems with the Law	1 2 3	4 5 6 7	8 9 10
Physical Health Problems	1 2 3	4 5 6 7	8 9 10

VI. MOTIVATION AND READINESS FOR TREATMENT

	LEVEL OF PROBLEM SEVERITY		
AREAS OF ASSESSMENT	**NONE OR LOW**	**MODERATE**	**HIGH**
Awareness of AOD Problem	1 2 3	4 5 6 7	8 9 10
Awareness DWI Problem	1 2 3	4 5 6 7	8 9 10
Acknowledge Need for Help	1 2 3	4 5 6 7	8 9 10
Willingness to Accept Help	1 2 3	4 5 6 7	8 9 10
Willingness for Level II Therapy	1 2 3	4 5 6 7	8 9 10
Have Taken Action to Change	1 2 3	4 5 6 7	8 9 10

I. ALCOHOL AND OTHER DRUG USE PROBLEM AREAS

PROBLEM AREA AND DESCRIPTION	CHANGES NEEDED IN THOUGHT AND ACTION	PROGRAMS AND RESOURCES TO BE USED TO MAKE CHANGES	DATES WORKED ON

II. IMPAIRED DRIVING PROBLEMS

PROBLEM AREA AND DESCRIPTION	CHANGES NEEDED IN THOUGHT AND ACTION	PROGRAMS AND RESOURCES TO BE USED TO MAKE CHANGES	DATES WORKED ON

III. THINKING FEELING, TRIGGERS AND ATTITUDE PATTERNS THAT LEAD TO DWI BEHAVIOR AND CONDUCT

PROBLEM AREA AND DESCRIPTION	CHANGES NEEDED IN THOUGHT AND ACTION	PROGRAMS AND RESOURCES TO BE USED TO MAKE CHANGES	DATES WORKED ON

IV. CURRENT LIFE SITUATION PROBLEMS

PROBLEM AREA AND DESCRIPTION	CHANGES NEEDED IN THOUGHT AND ACTION	PROGRAMS AND RESOURCES TO BE USED TO MAKE CHANGES	DATES WORKED ON

SESSION 3

PATHWAYS TO ALCOHOL

AND OTHER DRUG USE PROBLEM

OUTCOMES AND ADDICTION

OVERVIEW AND SESSION OBJECTIVES

OBJECTIVES OF THIS SESSION

▶ Review what we learned about alcohol and other drugs in **DWC Education**.

▶ Carefully review the Impaired Control Cycle or the mental-behavioral pathway to addiction.

▶ Learn another pathway to addiction: The mental-physical addiction cycle.

▶ Look at how genetics is related to addiction.

HERE IS WHAT WE LEARNED IN **DWC Education** about alcohol and other drugs (AOD).

▶ There are two kinds of drugs - drugs that speed you up (system enhancers) and drugs that slow you down (system suppressors).

▶ We build up a tolerance to certain kinds of drugs.

▶ Two drugs taken at the same time may cause one or both drugs to increase in strength.

▶ As the level of blood alcohol concentration (BAC) increases, the greater the impairment of judgment, behavior, emotions and brain functions. All of these have serious effects on driving behavior.

▶ BAC is affected by the number of drinks, your weight, how long you have been drinking, your gender, whether you have eaten and if you are fatigued or tired.

▶ Alcohol has a direct effect and impairs functioning or damages various parts of your body.

▶ There are health risks of AOD use.

▶ How various drugs affect our driving skills and behavior.

There are various patterns of AOD use and these can be used to define your own AOD use pattern.

▶ The pattern of quantity-frequency-prediction;

▶ The social patterns of solo and gregarious;

▶ The patterns of AOD use benefits; and

▶ The AOD use pattern that is high-risk for DWI behavior.

▶ Problem outcome patterns or misuse symptoms resulting from AOD use.

- **A drinking or other drug use problem:** anyone who has had a problem from AOD use will fit this pattern, including those who have received a DWI.

- **Problem drinker or drug user,** which is defined as a pattern of problems or negative outcomes.

- **Problem drinker (or drug user) who fits the diagnosis of Substance Abuse;** and

- **Problem drinker (or drug user) who fits the diagnosis of Substance Dependence.**

SESSION CONTENT AND FOCUS

There are two important impaired control pathways or cycles to AOD problem outcomes.

▶ The first pathway is the Mental-Behavior **Impaired Control Cycle (ICC).**
▶ The second pathway is the **Mental-Physical Impaired Control Cycle.**

We also call these pathways addiction cycles because they show how people develop mental and physical addiction to alcohol and other drugs. Many impaired drivers will not fit the full cycle of these two impaired control pathways. But parts of these two cycles will fit many, if not most, impaired drivers at one time in the past.

Keep an open mind as to how these pathways of impaired control use might apply to you.

You were referred to **DWC Therapy** because your evaluation showed you have experienced some problem outcomes from AOD use in the past that went beyond DWI behavior. Our purpose is to define the two pathways to AOD problem outcomes and give you an opportunity to see how you might fit these pathways and addiction cycles.

A. THE MENTAL-BEHAVIORAL IMPAIRED CONTROL CYCLE

The first step in developing AOD problem outcomes is when use becomes a **habit pattern.** This can lead to the IMPAIRED CONTROL CYCLE in *Figure 2,* page 43. For those who completed **DWC Education**, this will be a review.

▶ Life events (Point A in *Figure 2)* often lead to a need or desire to feel good (increase pleasure) or not feel bad (decrease discomfort). Drinking is one way to meet this **expectation** - Point B in *Figure 2.*
▶ Drinking does increase pleasure or decrease discomfort (our **appraisal:** it helps us cope). The thoughts about drinking and the drinking behavior are strengthened (Point C). Although many people never go beyond the Point A to C path, this path can lead to the AOD problem outcome cycle or the impaired-control cycle.
▶ As a result of drinking to feel good or to not feel bad, alcohol use leads to a problem - a drinking problem. **Let's have the problem be a DWI** - Point D in *Figure 2.* Many drinkers go no further in this cycle. They conclude "I've had a problem from drinking," **(appraisal),** "it's my fault" **(attribution),** and I'm never going to drink in such a way that I get another problem from drinking" **(decision). Such changes in thought lead to changes in action.**
▶ Getting a problem from drinking can lead to stress and discomfort. If drinking helps to cope with the life stresses, or to not feel bad - to relieve stress, then we would **expect** it will also help us deal with the stress that came from problems we got from drinking - say a DWI arrest. We drink to handle and cope with the stress that comes from drinking. This is Point E in our cycle. This sets the stage for the next step.

▶ The drinking we did to handle the problems from drinking leads to another problem - another DWI arrest, fight with our spouse, missing work. This is Point F in the cycle. This is a new problem. At point D, we said that we had a drinking problem. Now, we are far enough into the cycle to be called a *problem drinker.* We have developed a drinking problem pattern, a pattern of alcohol misuse. At this point, many drinkers **decide** to change the way they handle the problems of life and the problems from drinking. They change their thought and action habits. This leads to more adaptive ways to handle problems in life. *Figure 1*, page 14 in *Session 1* shows that this **action choice** can lead to positive outcomes.

▶ Some continue to use alcohol to handle the problems they get from drinking. Drinking habits resist change. Life situation problems that are not drinking related continue to occur. The problems from drinking have to be faced. They take another step in the *impaired control cycle* - drink to handle life problems and the additional problems from drinking. This is Point G in *Figure 2*.

▶ Further drinking leads to more problems, and this completes the AOD problem or addiction cycle. Now, the person drinks because he or she drinks. An old proverb sums it up: "A man takes the drink. The drink takes the drink. Then the drink takes the man."

▶ **We also call this impaired control cycle mental-behavioral addiction.**

Exercise: Use *Figure 2* as a Work Sheet to identify the specific ways you fit the various rectangles in the figure. For example, what are your life conditions or problems which lead you to drink alcohol (Rectangle A)? Write down under the rectangle what these are. Under rectangle B, write down your pattern of AOD use that helps you cope with your life stresses or problems. Continue to follow the cycle and write down how you fit each of the points in *Figure 2*.

B. THE MENTAL-PHYSICAL PATHWAY TO AOD PROBLEM OUTCOMES: THE PHYSICAL ADDICTION CYCLE

We will use alcohol to illustrate and describe the mental-physical addiction cycle as shown in Figure 3, page 44.

▶ First, alcohol and other drugs have a direct effect. As we learned in the *Mental-Behavioral Impaired Controlled Cycle,* people use alcohol for its direct effect. One drinks to feel relaxed, sedated, calm and to reduce mental and body stress.

▶ Second, the indirect or withdrawal effects from the drug are just the opposite. For alcohol, the indirect effect would be stress, agitation, anxiety and mental and body tension. We call this the rebound effect. This is shown in *Figure 3* below. Drinking produces the very condition for which the person drank in the first place.

▶ Third, one must now drink to cure the symptoms or the rebound effect from drinking. Mentally, you expect alcohol to do this. Physically and chemically, it does do this. To maintain a balance in body tension, you must continue to drink. Or, you must abstain long enough to work through the distressful condition of withdrawal, and develop a alcohol-free state of balance.

FIGURE 2

Mental-behavioral impaired control cycle (ICC).

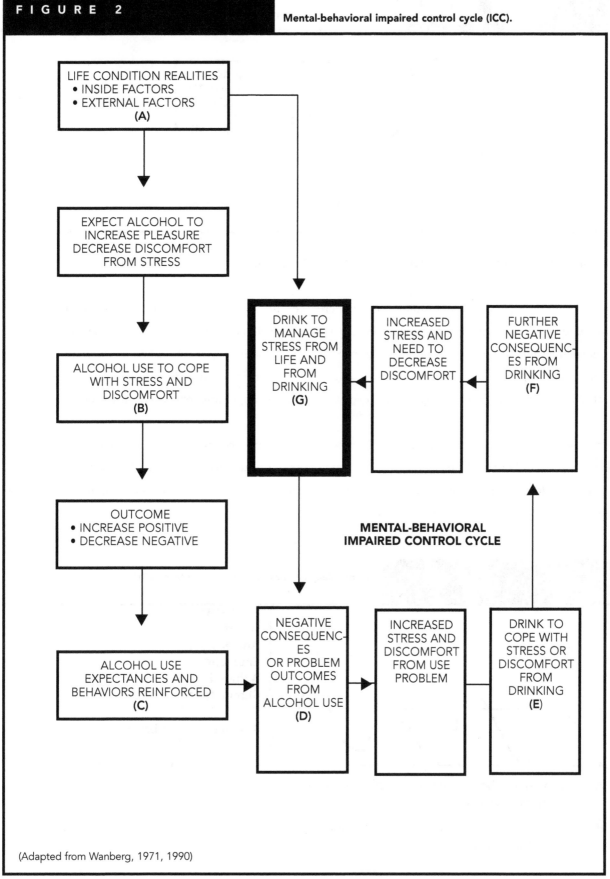

LIFE CONDITION REALITIES
• INSIDE FACTORS
• EXTERNAL FACTORS
(A)

EXPECT ALCOHOL TO
INCREASE PLEASURE
DECREASE DISCOMFORT
FROM STRESS

ALCOHOL USE TO COPE
WITH STRESS AND
DISCOMFORT
(B)

DRINK TO
MANAGE
STRESS FROM
LIFE AND
FROM
DRINKING
(G)

INCREASED
STRESS AND
NEED TO
DECREASE
DISCOMFORT

FURTHER
NEGATIVE
CONSEQUENC-
ES FROM
DRINKING
(F)

OUTCOME
• INCREASE POSITIVE
• DECREASE NEGATIVE

**MENTAL-BEHAVIORAL
IMPAIRED CONTROL CYCLE**

ALCOHOL USE
EXPECTANCIES AND
BEHAVIORS REINFORCED
(C)

NEGATIVE
CONSEQUENC-
ES
OR PROBLEM
OUTCOMES
FROM
ALCOHOL USE
(D)

INCREASED
STRESS AND
DISCOMFORT
FROM USE
PROBLEM

DRINK TO
COPE WITH
STRESS OR
DISCOMFORT
FROM
DRINKING
(E)

(Adapted from Wanberg, 1971, 1990)

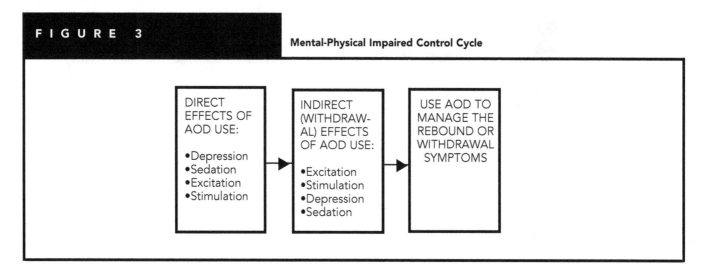

FIGURE 3 Mental-Physical Impaired Control Cycle

| DIRECT EFFECTS OF AOD USE: •Depression •Sedation •Excitation •Stimulation | → | INDIRECT (WITHDRAWAL) EFFECTS OF AOD USE: •Excitation •Stimulation •Depression •Sedation | → | USE AOD TO MANAGE THE REBOUND OR WITHDRAWAL SYMPTOMS |

The Mental-Physical Impaired Control Addiction Cycle is shown in *Figures 4 through 7*.

Figure 4 provides a picture of what might be the increased and decreased levels of nervous activity during our waking hours. The average tension level (ATL), (the nervous tension activity levels between lines A and B) would be a normal level of tension. When the level of nervous system activity goes above line A, we begin to feel some tension, irritation, agitation or noticeable levels of anxiety. When the activity level falls below line B, we begin to feel relaxed, tired, weak and sleepy. Each cycle in *Figure 4* is approximately two to three hours.

The high level of the cycle may be represented by both positive and negative types of stimulation. We could feel good and hyper and energetic; or we could feel agitated, anxious and tense. The kind of response we have at the high end will depend upon our mood, what is happening to us at the time and/or our emotional and physical needs.

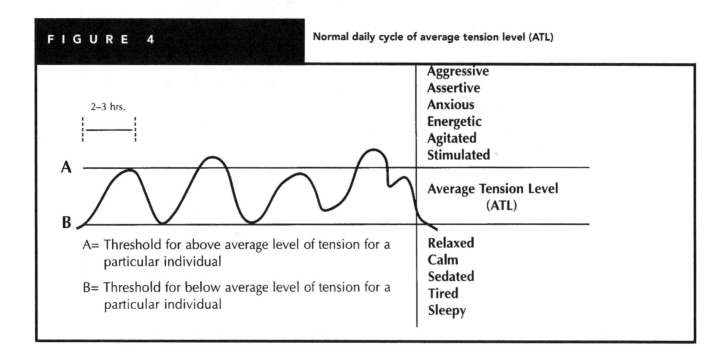

FIGURE 4 Normal daily cycle of average tension level (ATL)

Aggressive
Assertive
Anxious
Energetic
Agitated
Stimulated

Average Tension Level (ATL)

Relaxed
Calm
Sedated
Tired
Sleepy

2–3 hrs.

A= Threshold for above average level of tension for a particular individual

B= Threshold for below average level of tension for a particular individual

When we use a sedative drug such as alcohol, we slow down the nervous system. Alcohol will change the number of cycles and the level of activity in the nervous system activity cycle, as described in *Figure 5*. The body's reactions that take place with the suppressor (sedative) drugs, such as alcohol, are noted in the lower right-hand corner of *Figure 5*.

When alcohol begins to wear off, we begin to experience the "rebound" or nervous-excitement. This is the withdrawal or rebound reaction from the use of a sedative drug such as alcohol. The withdrawal effect is always longer than the sedative effect.

For example, if we take a drink at D1 *(Figure 5)*, we begin to experience a period of sedation for up to one to two hours that is followed by a period of rebound into stimulation and agitation that can last as long as three hours. A second drink taken about two hours later or at the peak of stimulation (D2) will have less of a sedative effect since it has to work against the body's rebound from the first drink. If we take a third drink at D3, or at the peak of the rebound from the first two drinks, then we will probably experience little sedative effect since that drink has to work against the body's rebound from the first two drinks.

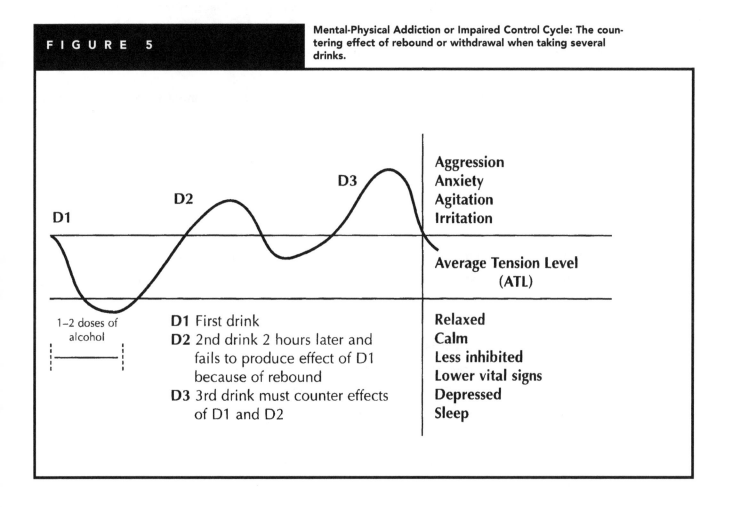

FIGURE 5

Mental-Physical Addiction or Impaired Control Cycle: The countering effect of rebound or withdrawal when taking several drinks.

D3

D2

D1

**Aggression
Anxiety
Agitation
Irritation**

**Average Tension Level
(ATL)**

1–2 doses of alcohol

D1 First drink
D2 2nd drink 2 hours later and fails to produce effect of D1 because of rebound
D3 3rd drink must counter effects of D1 and D2

**Relaxed
Calm
Less inhibited
Lower vital signs
Depressed
Sleep**

The rebound from sedation is the body's effort to keep from getting sedated. Sedation is the gradual slowing of the body's normal activity (heart beat, breathing) that, if allowed to continue, would result in the stopping of all of these normal activities. This is why, during sleep, we stay in deep sleep for only a short time; the body automatically springs back from this deep sedation since it is close to all activity stopping - or death. Thus, the natural reaction of the body to alcohol is to work against that drug to keep the body's activity from stopping. It does this by producing its own stimulant drugs. Because the external sedative drug, such as alcohol, is so strong, it overpowers these natural drugs. If we take enough alcohol, we will stop all activity and go into a coma and die.

The body must work against or *compensate* for this slowing down process. When the alcohol wears off, the natural drugs that worked against the alcohol take over (these are stimulant-like drugs). This is the basis for going into rebound, or a state of stimulation and agitation.

If we extend our drinking period, the body may have stored up larger amounts of its natural stimulant drug. The rebound may be more intense and occur over a longer period of time - many times longer than the period that we were sedated or drugged by alcohol. This is shown in *Figure 6,* page 47. Just how strong the rebound goes into the stress or agitation period will depend on how long and how much we drink. This is *drug withdrawal,* or the *abstinence syndrome.* It is the body's reaction to the drug leaving the system.

The rebound or withdrawal effect may continue for several weeks or even months following a longer period of alcohol use. Although the stimulation and agitation effects will most likely not be very intense, or even noticeable, the very presence of this agitation creates an ongoing level of stress. When this low level of stress is added to normal daily tension, stressful events are more difficult to handle. This may be one factor that causes relapses. One may be more vulnerable to relapsing during the several weeks or months following quitting drinking.

Taking a drink is one way to avoid the rebound symptoms or to "cure" the stress and agitation from withdrawal from alcohol. If one takes a drink at D2 in *Figure 6* this will "take off the edge." This is taking a "hair of the dog that bit you." It is one of the bases of addiction to alcohol.

A person who has developed a pattern of daily, steady drinking may need to drink every one or two hours during non-sleep periods to avoid the agitation of withdrawal and cure the rebound effect. This is the strung out user pictured in *Figure 7,* page 48. Doses of alcohol now spaced closely together must work against the rebound of prior doses. The rebound effect reduces the strength of each dose of alcohol.

This explains one reason why people become addicted to a drug. The body demands more of the drug to maintain the body balance (homeostasis) - the very drug that set off the state of nervous system imbalance. It is related to what the drug does to the nerve chemistry at the nerve endings themselves.

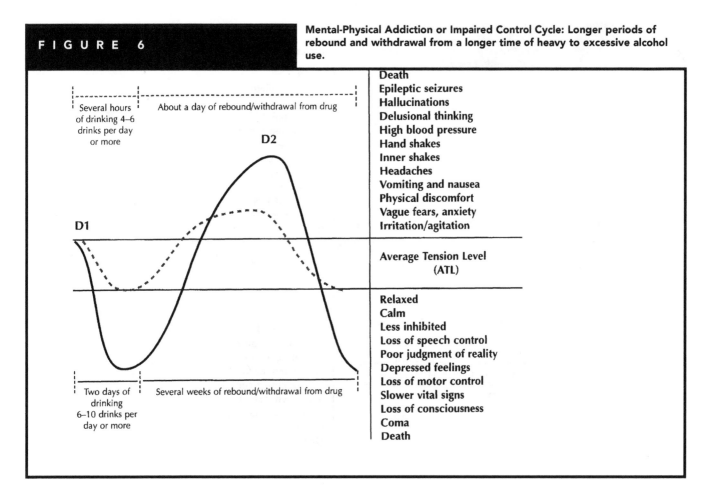

FIGURE 6

Mental-Physical Addiction or Impaired Control Cycle: Longer periods of rebound and withdrawal from a longer time of heavy to excessive alcohol use.

Several hours of drinking 4–6 drinks per day or more

About a day of rebound/withdrawal from drug

D2

D1

Two days of drinking 6–10 drinks per day or more

Several weeks of rebound/withdrawal from drug

Death
Epileptic seizures
Hallucinations
Delusional thinking
High blood pressure
Hand shakes
Inner shakes
Headaches
Vomiting and nausea
Physical discomfort
Vague fears, anxiety
Irritation/agitation

Average Tension Level
(ATL)

Relaxed
Calm
Less inhibited
Loss of speech control
Poor judgment of reality
Depressed feelings
Loss of motor control
Slower vital signs
Loss of consciousness
Coma
Death

A steady use of the drug may be for only the purpose of curing the discomfort of the rebound or withdrawal phase of use. If the drug is stopped after a period of use, minor symptoms such as inability to sleep, shakes or being irritable may occur within 24 hours. For the person who has been drinking steadily for several days to several weeks, more serious symptoms will begin to occur within 72 hours. These symptoms, given in the upper right-hand column of *Figure 7,* may be very serious and even life-threatening.

For many drugs, the effects of the rebound or withdrawal from a drug are the **opposite** of the direct or intoxicating effects of the drug. This addiction cycle can be applied to other drugs such as stimulants. The direct effects of a stimulant (amphetamine, cocaine) would be physical and mental excitability, stimulation or agitation. When the blood level of the stimulant drug drops, the rebound or withdrawal process begins and is the opposite of that for the sedative drugs or the suppressors. This rebound causes depression, tiredness, and we get what is called the "crashing" effect. The most effective short-term way to deal with these reactions is to re-engage in the use of the drug. Thus, the cocaine-addicted person begins to use cocaine to counteract the opposite or withdrawal effects of the cocaine.

In simple terms, mental-physical addiction is using the drug to "cure" the rebound or withdrawal from the drug. A continuous AOD user is essentially trying to avoid the mental and physical discomfort and pain of withdrawal.

Mental-physical Addiction or Impaired Control Cycle: The "strung out user"

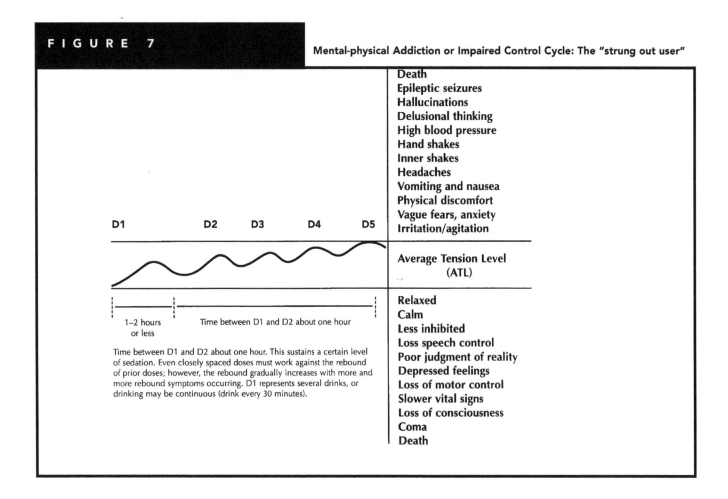

Death
Epileptic seizures
Hallucinations
Delusional thinking
High blood pressure
Hand shakes
Inner shakes
Headaches
Vomiting and nausea
Physical discomfort
Vague fears, anxiety
Irritation/agitation

Average Tension Level
(ATL)

Relaxed
Calm
Less inhibited
Loss speech control
Poor judgment of reality
Depressed feelings
Loss of motor control
Slower vital signs
Loss of consciousness
Coma
Death

D1   D2   D3   D4   D5

1–2 hours
or less   Time between D1 and D2 about one hour

Time between D1 and D2 about one hour. This sustains a certain level
of sedation. Even closely spaced doses must work against the rebound
of prior doses; however, the rebound gradually increases with more and
more rebound symptoms occurring. D1 represents several drinks, or
drinking may be continuous (drink every 30 minutes).

You may be saying, "I don't fit this mental-physical cycle. But look at *Figure 6,* page 47 again. This says that when you take two or three drinks within a couple of hours, you will rebound and experience mild agitation, stimulation or irritability. The body must withdraw from even two or three drinks. And this could last for a day. Most people who drink to a .05 to .08 BAC level (two to four drinks) will rebound once the BAC goes to zero.

After having several drinks in an evening, you may wake up in the middle of the night or early morning and can't go back to sleep. This is the rebound from those drinks. You woke up because your body was stimulated after being sedated by the alcohol. For some people, this happens quite often after having a few drinks. You might get a bit irritable after having several drinks and your BAC goes to zero. What other signs have you noticed after you have had several drinks and the alcohol wears off?

THE BODY MUST WITHDRAW FROM ALCOHOL EVEN AFTER ONE OR TWO DRINKS

Exercise: Using *Figure 3,* page 44, write down the direct results you get from alcohol (first Block in *Figure 3*). What are withdrawal or indirect results (second Block) that you might have had? Now, look at how *Figures 4 through 7* apply to you. Discuss this in group.

C. GENETIC FACTORS: IS ALCOHOLISM OR OTHER DRUG ADDICTION INHERITED?

▶ There appears to be no specific gene for alcoholism and for other types of drug addiction.

▶ There is a strong link between substance abuse and what is called the reward deficiency syndrome (RDS). Some people have lower amounts of some nerve chemicals, such as dopamine. This may cause a lack of feeling of well-being and an increase in feelings of anxiety. This may create a craving for substances that can provide this reward of well-being and take away the anxiety. The dopamine receptors can stimulate the brain's pleasure centers. Persons with a history of alcohol or cocaine addiction seem to lack these receptors. This seems to be based on genetics.

▶ If your parents had alcohol addiction problems, there is a greater chance that you may develop such addiction problems.

▶ Studies of twins compared with adopted children show that genetics increases the risk of alcoholism.

▶ Most research concludes that there are biological and genetic risk factors, yet, the psychological and social risk factors are very powerful in producing AOD abuse problems.

▶ The genetic factor is one of many that causes alcohol addiction - but one which does add to the risk.

D. CB (COGNITIVE-BEHAVIORAL) MAP EXERCISE

Exercise: Using *Figure 1,* page 14, and **Work Sheet 2**, page 21 as your guides, the group will do the CB MAP Exercise. One member will be asked to take a recent event that led to either a negative (bad) or positive (good) outcome. Describe that event and some automatic thoughts that followed the event. Describe the feelings and behaviors that followed those thoughts. What was the outcome? Then, the group member will be asked to identify the attitudes and beliefs underneath the thoughts. Most sessions will start with this CB MAP exercise. Make the focus of this session's CB MAP exercise "pressure from peers and friends to drink."

SESSION ACTIVITIES AND HOMEWORK

A. Update your Master Skills List and skills ratings, page 31.

B. Using *Work Sheet 6,* page 50, do a thinking report on an event that made you think you wanted to take a drink. Describe the event, your thoughts, feelings, beliefs and attitudes and the outcome.

C. Complete your *AOD Weekly Monitoring Chart* at the end of this *Workbook.*

CLOSURE PROCESS GROUP

Share with the group what you learned in this session.

Thinking report: Use an event that happened to you that made you think you wanted a drink.

THINKING REPORT

DESCRIBE THE EVENT:

YOUR THOUGHTS:

YOUR FEELINGS:

YOUR ATTITUDES AND BELIEFS:

THE OUTCOME:

SESSION 4

AOD PROBLEM OUTCOMES AND PATTERNS

YOUR RELAPSE AND RECIDIVISM PREVENTING GOALS

INTRODUCTION AND SESSION OBJECTIVES

IN THIS SESSION YOU ARE asked to look at the kinds of AOD problem symptoms you have had and what kind of problem outcome pattern you fit. You are also asked to write down your relapse prevention goal. This will be a review for those who completed DWC Education.

OBJECTIVES OF THIS SESSION

▶ Define your past problem outcome symptoms and see which problem outcome pattern you fit.

▶ Re-state your relapse prevention goal. Has this goal changed?

▶ See if your view of your alcohol/drug use patterns and problems have changed.

SESSION CONTENT AND FOCUS

As we disclose more about ourselves, we become more *self-aware.* As we become more self-aware, we change the views we have about ourselves. As we change our views of ourselves, we see the need to change our thinking and our behaviors. This is an important part of this program - first to change our views of ourselves, our thoughts and then our behaviors.

Our views of ourselves can only change if we continue to study ourselves and where we are now compared to where we were at some point in the past. Our work in this session will do just that. It is a reevaluation of how we see our past AOD problems and patterns. This will then allow us to have a more realistic view of where we are now and will give us clues of what we need to change.

A. RELATING YOUR PROBLEM OUTCOME PATTERNS TO YOUR MASTER PROFILE AND MASTER ASSESSMENT PLAN

Use the *Alcohol and Other Drug Use Assessment* part of your *Master Profile* when looking at your problem outcome patterns in this session. You may want to add to your *Master Assessment Plan* at the end of this session to see if you have listed all of the alcohol and other drug use problem areas.

B. IDENTIFYING YOUR PROBLEM OUTCOME SYMPTOMS AND PATTERNS

In **DWC Education,** you evaluated yourself as to whether you have ever had any AOD problem outcome symptoms. You were also asked to determine what pattern of problem outcome you might fit. We will do this once again.

Exercise: *Using Work Sheet 7,* page 55, check which drugs you have used, and for each of those drugs, check any of the problem outcomes, consequences or symptoms that you ever had from using that drug. Even if a symptom only happened once, still check it.

Exercise: *Using Work Sheet 8,* page 57, check whether any of the statements that describe *Substance Abuse* apply to you.

Exercise: *Using Work Sheet 9,* page 57, check whether you have ever fit any of the statements that describe *Substance Dependence.*

Exercise: *Using Work Sheet 10,* page 58, check whether you fit any of the classes of AOD problem outcomes that have ever applied to you. If you checked *Substance Use Dependence,* then you would have checked all of the other three categories. Discuss your findings in your closure process group.

If you did this in **DWC Education,** has your view of yourself changed? In the space below, write how your view of yourself as to problem outcome symptoms and patterns has changed. Discuss this in your process group.

HOW HAS YOUR VIEW OF YOURSELF CHANGED?

C. YOUR RELAPSE PREVENTION GOAL

Let's give some further thought about your *relapse prevention goal.* Remember, OUR GOALS ALWAYS GUIDE OUR ACTIONS. You have been asked to consider two personal commitment goals with respect to your use of alcohol and other drugs.

▶ **Personal Commitment Goal I:** To prevent alcohol from causing harm to you or others or upsetting and disturbing your life and/or the lives of others. This goal indicates that you may choose to continue to drink alcohol, but you are committing yourself to a non-harmful pattern of use or to a plan that would prevent your involvement in a pattern of use that causes you or others problems or harm.

▶ **Personal Commitment Goal II:** To live alcohol and drug free - preventing AOD use from causing harm to myself or others by abstaining from the use of alcohol or other mind and behavioral altering drugs.

We expect you to abstain from all illegal drug use. **WE DO NOT WANT TO GIVE YOU THE IMPRESSION THAT IT IS OK TO USE ILLEGAL-ILLICIT DRUGS. IT IS NOT OK.** As to illegal drugs, we would want you to adopt **Personal Commitment Goal II - TO NOT USE.** But alcohol is a different story since it is legal for persons 21 or older.

If you fit the *Alcohol Abuse or Alcohol Dependence* category, then we strongly recommend you choose PERSONAL COMMITMENT II - ABSTINENCE. We ask you to give that CAREFUL thought.

Now, has your relapse prevention goal changed? It might be something different than one of the two personal relapse prevention goals above. Write it in the space below.

MY PERSONAL RELAPSE PREVENTION GOAL

SESSION AND HOMEWORK ACTIVITIES

A. Update your master Skills List and ratings, page 31.

B. Using *Work Sheet 11,* page 58, do a thinking report on an event that happened to you that challenged your *Personal Commitment Relapse Prevention Goal.* Describe the event, your thoughts, feelings, beliefs, attitudes and outcome.

C. Before coming to group next week, complete your *AOD Weekly Monitoring Chart.* Check whether you thought about drinking or using drugs. Did you use, did you think about driving after you used and did you drive after using alcohol or other drugs?

CLOSURE PROCESS GROUP

Discuss your relapse prevention goal. Why did you choose that goal?

DRUG TYPE	PROBLEM CONSEQUENCES AND SYMPTOMS
ALCOHOL Beer Wine Spirits	Loss of verbal control Loss of behavioral control Impairment of judgment Irresponsible behavior to others Irresponsible behavior to community Physical violence Self-harm behavior Blackouts, passing out Disturbs heart rate, sweats, panic Disturbs body rhythm (sleep) Suspicious distrust of others Accidents and injuries Shakes and tremors, vomiting Convulsions and seizures Hallucinations, delusional thinking Neglect family, work, school Financial problems Break the law Body organ damage and impairment Impairs driving ability Physical/psychological dependence Tolerance
CANNIBUS Marijuana Hash	Mental confusion Distorts reality Overdose can cause psychotic states Decreases motivation Decreases normal interests Impairs short-term memory Increases heart rate Can impair reproductive ability Decreases abstract thinking Causes suspicious distrust Hallucinations in large doses Tolerance Psychological dependence Increases risk of lung diseases
STIMULANTS Cocaine Metamphetamine Amphetamines Ecstasy (MDA)	Rapid heartbeat, breathing Sweating, headaches, insomnia Impairs heart rhythm large doses Nausea, vomiting Restless, agitation, moody Weight loss Impairs judgment Impairs responsibility to others Impairs social functioning Hallucinations, delusions, paranoia Muscle weakness Mental confusion, seizures Depression, fatigue, agitation, oversleeping, suicidal thinking on withdrawal from stimulants Tolerance Physical/psychological dependence

DRUG TYPE	PROBLEM CONSEQUENCES AND SYMPTOMS
DEPRESSANTS Barbiturates Methaqualone Tranquilizers	Impaired psychological functioning Slurred speech, incoordination Impaired memory and attention Impaired social functioning Impaired judgment Stupor, coma Staggering and stumbling Slow heart beat, breathing Withdrawal: hyper, sweating, seizures, anxiety, agitation, tremors, vomiting, rapid heart beat, insomnia Tolerance Physical/psychological dependence
HALLUCINOGENS LSD Phencyclidine (PCP) Mescaline Peyote Mushrooms	Impairs responsibility to others Distorts reality, senses Panic, violence Anxiety, depression Hallucinations, delusions Suspicious distrust, paranoia Impaired social functioning Disturbs body functions: sweating, tremors, rapid heartbeat Tolerance Convulsions, coma Flashbacks after stop use
INHALANTS Nitrous oxide Amyl nitrate Paint Gas	Impaired memory or attention Drowsiness or coma Slurred speech Reduced hunger, thirst, sex drive Stop breathing Malnutrition, infection, hepatitis Tiredness, loss judgment Loss of self-control Painful withdrawal: depression, vomiting, muscle aches, diarrhea, fever, unable to sleep Dependence, addiction
OPIATES Heroin Morphine Codeine	Impaired social functioning Impaired psychological functioning Apathy Depression Sleepiness, coma Impaired memory, attention Slurred speech Physical withdrawal: vomiting, muscle aches, drippy nose, sweating, fever, insomnia

Risk for diagnosis of Substance Abuse taken from the Diagnostic and Statistical Manual IV. Check the right column if they happened to you within the same 12 month time period.

RULES OR CRITERIA FOR DIAGNOSIS OF SUBSTANCE ABUSE	CHECK
1. Repeated substance use causing a failure to live up to the major role duties at work, school, or home (such as repeatedly missing work or poor work output or performances related to AOD use, AOD related absences, AOD related suspensions or being expelled from school, neglecting your household duties or children).	
2. Repeated AOD use in situations where it is dangerous (such as driving or operating a machine when AOD impaired).	
3. Repeated AOD-related legal problems (such as several DWI, AOD-related disorderly conduct, charges related to domestic violence).	
4. Continue AOD use knowing that you have had repeated or persistent social or relationship problems caused by or made worse by AOD use (such as arguments with a spouse over consequences of intoxication, physical fights, etc.).	

Risk for diagnosis of Substance Dependence taken from the Diagnostic and Statistical Manual IV. Check the right column if they happened to you within the same 12 month time period.

RULES OR CRITERIA FOR DIAGNOSIS OF SUBSTANCE DEPENDENCE	CHECK
1. Your tolerance has changed in either of the following ways: a) a need for a marked or obvious increase or raised amounts of substances to get the same level of desired effect or intoxication b) marked decrease or drop in effect with continued use of the same amount of substances.	
2. You have had signs or symptoms of withdrawal from AOD use as shown by the following: a) showing a withdrawal syndrome or pattern when stopping the use of a substance, such as: sweating, increased pulse rate, shakes, unable to sleep, sick to stomach, seeing, hearing or feeling things not there, feeling anxious, having a convulsion or seizure; b) when the substance is taken to relieve or avoid the symptoms of withdrawal.	
3. When you have taken the substance in larger amounts over a longer period of time than you really meant to or what you intended.	
4. When you have had a desire to cut down or control the use or you have been unable to cut down, control or stop using the substance.	
5. You have spent a great deal of time in doing things to get substances (driving to get liquor late at night, driving long distances to a bar or liquor store, making sure you would always have your afternoon drinks), or use the substance or to recover from its use.	
6. You have given up important and enjoyable social, work or recreational activities or reduce these activities so that you can drink or use drugs.	
7. You continue to use alcohol or other drugs even though you know its use has caused you repeated or recurring problems (continue to drive even though you know you can get or have gotten a DWI, continue to drink even though you know it will upset your spouse or cause you to get into conflicts with your spouse).	

AOD use problem classes. Now rate yourself as to what classes of AOD use problems you fit into. Check all that apply.

AOD USE PROBLEM CLASSES: CHECK ALL THAT FIT YOU	YES	NO
1. *Drinking or Other Drug Use Problem:* If you have ever had a problem from AOD Use, then check yes. If you see getting a DWI as being a problem, then you have an AOD use problem. If you checked any symptom in *Work Sheet 7*, you have had an *AOD problem*.		
2. *Problem Drinker or Problem Drug User:* If you have had several AOD use problems for a period of time or during your lifetime, then you have been into a pattern of alcohol or other drug use. We call this *problem drinking* or *problem drugging*. If you check several symptoms in *Work Sheet 7*, you are probably a problem drinker.		
3. *Problem Drinker or User - AOD Abuse:* You fit this category if you have had several AOD use problems for a period of time or during your life and you checked one of the statements in *Work Sheet 8*, you fit this category.		
4. *Alcohol or Other Drug Dependence:* You fit this category if you have had repeated problems from AOD use and if you check three or more of the statements in *Work Sheet 9*. If you fit this category, you fit the above three categories.		

Thinking report: Event that challenged your relapse prevention goal

THINKING REPORT
DESCRIBE THE EVENT:
YOUR THOUGHTS:
YOUR FEELINGS:
YOUR ATTITUDES AND BELIEFS:
THE OUTCOME:

S E S S I O N 5

MANAGING AOD CRAVINGS

AND URGES

OVERVIEW AND SESSION OBJECTIVES

IF YOU HAVE BEEN using alcohol or other drugs in a consistent way, and since you have stopped using, you may have cravings - or the desire to use drugs. The purpose of this session will be to look at cravings and urges and to develop strategies to handle them.

OBJECTIVES OF THIS SESSION

▶ Understand cravings and urges.

▶ Develop skills to cope with cravings and urges.

We will begin this session by:

▶ Going over this week's thinking report - an event that challenged your relapse prevention goal: and

▶ Doing the CB MAP exercise.

SESSION CONTENT AND FOCUS

A. RELATING CRAVINGS AND URGES TO YOUR MASTER PROFILE AND MASTER ASSESSMENT PLAN

If you rated yourself moderate to high on alcohol or on another drug *and* on the *Sustained or Continuous Scale* of your *Master Profile,* then you may struggle with AOD cravings and urges. Should cravings and urges be on your problem list in your *Master Assessment Plan?*

B. WHAT IS A CRAVING OR AN URGE?

A craving is the wanting or desire to drink, to get drunk or use drugs. Cravings can be uncomfortable but last a short time. The problem is, they can move into urges. An urge is moving towards fulfilling the craving. **It is alcohol-drug seeking behavior.**

Often, the basis of our craving is *anxiety.* Something is bothering us. Rather than looking at what is bothering us, we have urges and cravings.

Cravings may be triggered by some event that happens to you - a high-risk situation: being around friends who use; going to a party where there is alcohol; a high- stress situation. But the craving may trigger an urge. Urges may cause physical symptoms such as nervousness, tightness in the stomach and/or psychological symptoms such as positive memories of being high or socializing over a drink. Urges peak quickly and then drop off. You can stop the urge by stopping the craving. If you have an urge, stop the action that goes with the urge. **Craving is mental; the urge is an action towards fulfilling the craving.**

C. WHAT CAN TRIGGER CRAVINGS AND URGES OR AOD SEEKING BEHAVIORS?

▶ Being around alcohol and other drugs.

▶ Memories about the fun and "good" times you had when drinking.

▶ Seeing other people using.

▶ Being with people who are drinking or using drugs.

▶ Certain emotions, including fatigue, stress, self-doubt, nostalgia, anger, frustration, excitement or accomplishment.

▶ Desire for drinking environments - bars, parties.

D. SOME WAYS TO COPE WITH CRAVINGS AND URGES

▶ Finding another activity that will distract you from the craving or urge or from seeking alcohol or drinking environments.

▶ Talking to family or friends about the cravings or urges.

▶ "Toughing it out" or "urge surfing" and getting control of the craving by bearing the discomfort. It will go away with time. Here is how you do it.

- What are your thoughts and feelings about the craving? WHAT ARE YOU ANXIOUS ABOUT?
- Is it still a craving? Or is it now an urge? If you feel it in your body and you are now taking action to fulfill the craving or seek alcohol or other drugs - like going to the liquor store, or calling an old buddy you used to drink with - it is an urge. Remember: Cravings are mental; urges move you to action.
- When you feel the craving become an urge, focus on where in your body you feel the urge. Use self-talk skills. Talk down the urge. "Turn the corner." Talk to a non-using friend instead of going to the liquor store. The urge will go away faster than you think. But TURN THE CORNER.
- Your craving may be nothing more than a desire to be in a drinking environment.

▶ Think about:

- The bad things that have happened to you because of your AOD use - such as your DWI arrest, ending up in jail, losing money. Make a list of these.
- Make a list of the rewards of being AOD-free or of not being in a problem using pattern.

▶ Stop and think.

- What do you have to lose by relapsing back into a pattern of problem use and abuse?
- What do you have to lose by going back to impaired driving and getting another DWI?

Exercise: Now do *Work Sheet 12,* page 63.

E. PRACTICE MANAGING A CRAVING OR URGE USING COGNITIVE CHANGE SKILLS

▶ Choose an episode of craving such as a desire to get drunk or get high. What are the thoughts behind the craving?

▶ Use *thought stopping* and *countering*. Try *shifting the view*. How do these work?

▶ What was the *self-talk* you used in managing the craving?

▶ Were you managing a craving or an urge? It is much harder to deal with the urge. Try to stop the craving before it moves to an urge.

Exercise: Use *Work Sheet 13,* page 63 - *Dealing with Cravings and Urges.* The plan you make up for this exercise can help you deal with cravings and urges you may get down the road.

F. DO ANOTHER CB MAP EXERCISE

▶ For this CB MAP Exercise, someone will choose an event that sets off a craving for something; alcohol, chocolate, coffee, drugs. Remember, the urge is the **seeking behavior.**

▶ Use *Figure 1,* page 14 as your MAP.

SESSION AND HOMEWORK ACTIVITIES

A. Add to and update your Master Skills list, page 31.

B. Using *Work Sheet 14,* page 64, do a thinking report on an event that happened to you that caused you to have a desire for a drink or to get drunk. Describe the event, your thoughts, your feelings, your beliefs and attitudes and the outcome.

C. Before coming to group next week, complete your *AOD Weekly Monitoring Chart.* Check whether you thought about drinking or using drugs, whether you were in a situation where alcohol and/or drugs were being used. Did you use? If you used, did you think about driving after you used and did you drive after using alcohol or other drugs?

CLOSURE PROCESS GROUP

Discuss cravings and urges you have had. Describe your AOD seeking behaviors.

Joys and Pleasures. What are your joys and pleasures and would you lose them if you relapsed into a pattern of AOD problem use or if you received another DWI arrest?

LIST 8 PLEASURES AND JOYS THAT YOU HAVE IN YOUR LIFE. MAKE THESE YOUR TOP PLEASURES AND JOYS:	WOULD YOU LOSE THEM IF YOU GOT ANOTHER DWI OR RELAPSED?	
	YES	NO

Dealing With Cravings. Make up a plan to deal with an episode of craving. Pick two or three of the strategies suggested in class and detail how you would use them when you have a strong urge to drink or use other drugs.

Describe your episode of a strong desire to have a drink or to get drunk.

What mental skills could you use? Thought stopping? Shifting the view?

What social skills could you use? Could you call a friend? Talk with your intimate partner?

What physical skills could you use? Go for a walk? Go to the gym and work out?

Thinking report: Use an event that happened to you to that made you think you wanted a drink.

THINKING REPORT

DESCRIBE THE EVENT:

YOUR THOUGHTS:

YOUR FEELINGS:

YOUR ATTITUDES AND BELIEFS:

THE OUTCOME:

SESSION 6

SKILLS IN COGNITIVE SELF-CONTROL

RECOGNIZING AND CHANGING NEGATIVE THOUGHTS AND NEGATIVE THINKING

OVERVIEW AND SESSION OBJECTIVES

THIS IS ONE of four sessions that will focus on developing skills for cognitive self-control. We first look at how negative thoughts and attitudes influence our lives. Then we will learn to identify negative thinking and skills to change our negative thoughts.

OBJECTIVES OF THIS SESSION

▶ Review the model for the process of learning and change in Figure 1.

▶ Understand how negative thinking affects our lives and to recognize our negative thought patterns.

▶ Recognize how negative thought patterns contribute to problem behaviors.

▶ Apply cognitive change tools to change negative thinking.

We will begin this session by:

▶ Going over this week's thinking report on an event that made you think you wanted to drink;

▶ Doing the CB MAP exercise.

SESSION CONTENT AND FOCUS

A. DOES YOUR MASTER PROFILE INDICATE YOU HAVE PROBLEMS WITH NEGATIVE THINKING?

Look at your ratings on the *Assessment of Thinking, Feeling and Attitude Patterns.* Many of the items would indicate negative thinking. Update your MAP (Master Assessment Plan).

B. HOW NEGATIVE THINKING AFFECTS OUR LIVES

THE WAY WE THINK CONTROLS HOW WE FEEL AND ACT. *Negative thinking* can become a way of life. It can lead to negative and angry behavior.

Negative thoughts lead to negative emotions and to tension. "The world sucks!" When we believe that, we believe that the world doesn't deserve anything positive. It makes it easier to "do what you want," regardless of how it might affect people.

Negative thinking can lead to negative feelings about oneself, to anger and depression. *Negative thinking* usually works against positive outcomes. It works against your goals and what you want to accomplish. It throws a damper on feeling good.

C. RECOGNIZING NEGATIVE THOUGHTS AND THINKING

Before you can change negative thoughts you have to recognize them. They can be errors in thinking. Here are some errors in thinking that are negative thoughts.

▶ **Expecting the worst:** The worst always happens. "I know it won't work out."
▶ **Self-putdowns and self-blame:** "I'm no good." "I deserve it."
▶ **Expect yourself and others to be perfect:** "I should have done better."
▶ **Jumping to conclusions:** "I'm going to get fired."
▶ **Castastrophizing:** "I know something terrible is going to happen."
▶ **Magnifying:** "No matter what may happen, it couldn't be worse."

Exercise: Using *Work Sheet 15,* page 69, in column 1, list negative thoughts that you get into. Then, in column 2, label what kind of thinking errors these are, using the list above or the list of errors in thinking in *Worksheet 19, Session 7,* page 77.

D. NEGATIVE THINKING CAN LEAD TO RECIDIVISM (DRIVING WHILE IMPAIRED) AND ALCOHOL OR OTHER DRUG USE

▶ Think about the times that you went out and drank too much. Did you have some angry or negative thoughts? Maybe you were angry at someone close to you. Did you think, "screw them, I don't care"?
▶ **Exercise:** Use *Work Sheet 16,* page 70. List negative thoughts that you had before you drank too much or when driving after drinking.

E. THE STEPS AND SKILLS IN CHANGING NEGATIVE THINKING

You are in control of what you think or say to yourself. You may say "I had no choice, they made me do it." But you always have a choice of your thoughts and actions.

When we change our negative thoughts, we experience power. The power comes in using skills to control negative thinking. There is power in positive thinking. The power is *becoming more self-skilled.* This gives us greater self-mastery or *self-efficacy.*

Here are the steps to change *negative thinking.*

▶ Notice the *negative thinking.*
▶ Tell yourself that your *negative thinking* is irrational, foolish, not sensible.
▶ Use these two mental skills.

- **Thought stopping:** Allow yourself to think a negative thought. Then tell yourself to STOP the thought. Choose one target negative thought. (e.g., "nothing works out.") Every time that happens: BE AWARE! STOP THE THOUGHT!

- **Positive thought planting:** Pick a target negative thought. Every time you have that thought, replace it with a positive thought.

▶ **Use Positive Thought Arming:** Arm yourself with positive thoughts. It's having the thought and action there ready to use. Use *Work Sheet 17,* page 71 to make a list of positive thoughts you can use to arm yourself. Here are some examples.

- *Remember the good things:* What are the good things in life, the people that you care about?
- *Statements of hope:* Make positive self statements: "I can handle this."
- *Self-rewards:* When you have done something well, reward yourself with positive self-talk. "I came close to using, but I found another way to cope. I did a good job controlling myself." The key to change is rewarding yourself when you have made the change.
- *Always remember,* one of the most positive thoughts you can have is to know you can change your negative thoughts and feelings to those that lead to positive outcomes. **There is power in this.**

F.   IT'S ABOUT SELF-TALK

What we are doing is talking to ourselves. When you replace a negative thought, you are telling yourself to do this. This is self-talk and it is powerful. It can also be negative and irrational. Our goal is to *replace negative self-talk with positive self-talk.*

G. <u>EXERCISES</u>

▶ Using *Work Sheet 18,* page 72, do a Re-thinking Report. Follow the instructions for *Work Sheet 18.*

▶ Update your Master Skills List, page 31. Look over the skills you have worked on. Update your ratings.

HOMEWORK AND CLOSURE PROCESS GROUP

A. Do your *AOD Weekly Monitoring Chart* in the Appendix of this *Participant's Workbook.*

B. Discuss some of the negative thoughts you have had in your life that have led to bad outcomes.

List of negative thoughts and kind of error in thinking.

LIST NEGATIVE THOUGHTS	WHAT KIND OF ERROR IN THINKING

List negative thoughts that you had before you drank too much or before you drove after you were drinking.

NEGATIVE THOUGHTS THAT YOU HAD BEFORE DRINKING TOO MUCH	NEGATIVE THOUGHTS THAT YOU HAD WHEN DRIVING WHILE IMPAIRED

Positive thought arming: Make a list of positive thoughts that you can use. This is arming yourself with positive thoughts. Repeat these thoughts to yourself. Use *self-talk* in practicing these positive thoughts. Each time this week you get into a negative thought, pull out one of these positive thoughts on your list.

WORKSHEET 18

Re-thinking report to change negative thinking: Take a situation that usually leads to negative thinking. Re-think the event and change the thoughts to positive ones. What are the feelings now? What beliefs do you need to have to support the positive thoughts? Will it lead to a different outcome?

1. DESCRIBE AN EVENT OR SITUATION THAT LEADS TO NEGATIVE THINKING - MAYBE YOUR JOB.

2. RE-THINK THE EVENT AND WRITE SOME POSITIVE THOUGHTS ABOUT THAT SITUATION.

3. WHAT NEW FEELINGS COME WITH THE POSITIVE THINKING?

4. WHAT NEW BELIEFS MUST YOU HAVE TO SUPPORT THOSE POSITIVE THOUGHTS AND FEELINGS?

5. WILL THE OUTCOME BE MORE POSITIVE? WRITE THAT OUTCOME DOWN.

SESSION 7

SKILLS IN COGNITIVE SELF-CONTROL

RECOGNIZING AND CHANGING

ERRORS IN THINKING

OVERVIEW AND SESSION OBJECTIVES

OUR ATTITUDES, beliefs and thinking patterns have often led to bad outcomes. They can be barriers to change. Our goal is to change the thinking and behaviors that have led to bad outcomes and replace them with correct or rewarding ideas. We want to replace them with beliefs that can lead us to a satisfying lifestyle.

One set of thoughts and beliefs are our *errors in logic or our distorted beliefs* about ourselves and the world. Our thought patterns or thought habits (automatic thoughts) about the outside world and about ourselves can become twisted and distorted. We call these errors in logic or errors in thinking. We will take a closer look at errors in thinking in this session.

OBJECTIVES FOR THIS SESSION:

▶ Recognize distorted thinking patterns (thought-habits) and begin to change those thinking habits.

▶ Understand how these errors in thinking can lead to bad or undesirable outcomes.

SESSION CONTENT AND FOCUS

A. REVIEW AND UPDATE

▶ **Look at your work on the AOD Weekly Monitoring Chart.** Have you thought about drinking over the past few weeks? Have you had lapses?

▶ **Review and update your Master Profile.** How do you see yourself now. Look over your ratings. Do you see yourself as having higher ratings on some MP scales? Change those on which you now see yourself differently.

▶ **Review and update your Master Assessment Plan (MAP).** Are there problems you need to add to the MAP? Your counselor will update your individual treatment plan (ITP).

▶ **Your group will also review the CB MAP, Figure 1, page 14 and some parts of that MAP.**

- **Automatic thoughts** follow events that take place outside of us or inside of us. They may be expectations, appraisals, attributions and decisions. They are thought habits.
- **Attitudes** are thoughts for or against ideas, persons or objects in our life. It is the position we take towards the outside world. They are hooked into feelings. They are positive or negative.
- **Beliefs** are our values, ideas and principles we use to evaluate other people, ourselves and the world. They bond us to ourselves and the outside world. Our thoughts, attitudes and beliefs control how we react to people and events in our everyday life.

▶ **CB MAP exercise.** Use Figure 1, page 14, and Work Sheet 2, page 21, as guides.

B. UNDERSTANDING AND DEFINING THINKING ERRORS

▶ **A thinking error is a mistaken or distorted thought or view of situations, of ourselves or of the outside world.** It is not a genuine or valid understanding or explanation of what is really going on.

▶ **Look again at your MP.** If you rated yourself high on the questions in the Assessment of Thinking, Feeling and Attitude Patterns of your Master Profile, you may be using a lot of errors in thinking or logic.

▶ **Here are some common thought habits that are errors in thinking.**

• **"I had no choice."** It is one of the most commonly used excuses for doing something that leads to negative outcomes.

• **"Everybody does it."** This thinking puts up "road blocks to change." It may seem that "everyone drinks," but 30 percent of Americans do not drink alcohol. Or, "everybody drives when they have had too much to drink." Is this true?

• **"I'm right and my thoughts don't need changing."** Stubborn refusal to think differently may get you into trouble. There is no issue in the world where there isn't another way to think about it. Don't let stubbornness be a barrier to change.

• **"I have something coming. I deserve better than this."** This is the "entitlement trap." We will take a closer look at this later.

▶ **Write in the space below the most common thinking errors of impaired drivers.**

THE MOST COMMON THINKING ERRORS OF IMPAIRED DRIVERS

C. CORRECTING THINKING ERRORS THAT GET US INTO TROUBLE

▶ Errors in thinking are distortions that we do as a matter of habit. They become so automatic that we accept them even if we have no facts to support what we think.

▶ **Exercise:** *Work Sheet 19,* page 77 gives you a list of thinking errors. Practice changing those thinking errors. First check those that you use at least sometimes. Then write down a correction to that error. If you use: POWER THRUST - "I'm better than others." You might correct that with: "Some people are better than I am in many areas." Now, practice the skill of thought stopping to block thinking errors.

▶ **Exercise:** Use the thought change skill "shifting the view." Take the error in thinking: "I feel I've been screwed." *Shift the view.* Use statements which change that view. Try this: "There have been some people who have helped me and not 'screwed' me." Now shift the view on other thinking errors in *Work Sheet 19.*

D. THE "ENTITLEMENT TRAP"

We often use entitlement as a way to excuse or explain our actions that cause problem outcomes. Because of past problems and hurts which you think were beyond your control, you may think or feel you were the victim. You may think you were punished, deprived, badly treated. This merely makes you think you have something coming. You might even take this attitude into your relationships with people close to you such as your intimate partner. This attitude may prevent you from being responsible to others and to your community. You may have used this as a way to excuse your DWI behavior. Here is a story told by someone who was in alcohol treatment. He was never caught for impaired driving.

"I went through a tough divorce. It's been almost five years. Haven't found anyone I can trust. My kids won't talk to me. Just like my dad did to me. He wouldn't talk to me. My mom died when I was nine. Sure, I've been drinking too much. But I felt I deserved it. Been driving too, when I drink. But I take my chances. I think I've felt I got this much coming. Going to the bar is the one thing I've looked forward to."

Exercise: Use the self-talk skill of "think of the other person's position." Think of a thought that falls into the "entitlement trap" class. Now, think of the other person's position. *Example:* "I have a right to stay here and drink the way she's treated me." Think of her position. "She hasn't been feeling good. She needs my support. I'm going home."

Think of the other drivers who were on the road when you drove impaired. Were you putting them at risk? Put yourself in their position. Did you think that you were entitled to drive impaired? What are your thoughts now about the times you drove impaired? Share these in your closure group.

SESSION AND HOMEWORK ACTIVITIES

A. Update your Master Skills list and skills ratings, page 31.

B. Using *Work Sheet 20,* page 78 do a thinking report on the "entitlement trap." Take a situation or event where you thought you had something coming. What were your thoughts, feelings, beliefs and outcome?

C. Do your *AOD Weekly Monitoring Chart* before coming to session next week.

CLOSURE PROCESS GROUP

Talk about how you have used the *entitlement trap.* Share with your group some of your errors in thinking that may have led to bad outcomes or problems for you.

Checklist for identifying your errors in thinking.

ERRORS IN THINKING	CHECK IF YOU USE	CORRECT THIS THINKING ERROR BY WRITING A CORRECTIVE STATEMENT
POWER THRUST: Better than others		
ZERO STATE: Feeling of no value		
VICTIM STANCE: Blaming others, poor me		
PRIDE: Had no choice		
DON'T CARE: Lack concern how others affected		
PARANOID: Everybody is out to get me		
DISTRUST: Can't depend or trust anyone		
DEMAND: I want it right now		
SOLO: Don't need help		
PROCRASTINATE: I don't have to do it now		
STUBBORN: Won't change my ideas or give in, no way		
RIGID: Think in black and white terms		
CATASTROPHIZE: Mountains out of mole hills, the worst will happen		
PICKED ON: Feel singled out		
JUST DESERTS: They deserve it or have it coming		
FAIR DESERTS: I deserve more than what I'm getting		
CHEATED: I was shortchanged, didn't get what I had coming		
SCREWED: Feeling mistreated		
MAGNIFY: Blow things out of proportion		
WEAK: Can't stand up to what is best for yourself		
LYING: Exaggerating the truth, almost automatic for you		
HOSTILE: Everyone does it		

Thinking report: Use an event or situation where you thought you had something coming - "the entitlement trap."

THINKING REPORT

DESCRIBE THE EVENT:

YOUR THOUGHTS:

YOUR FEELINGS:

YOUR ATTITUDES AND BELIEFS:

THE OUTCOME:

SESSION 8

SKILLS IN COGNITIVE SELF-CONTROL

MANAGING EMOTIONS, STRESS
AND DEPRESSION

INTRODUCTION AND SESSION OBJECTIVES

FOR THE PERSON WHO USES ALCOHOL, stress is a two-edged sword. First, stress is an important reason why people use alcohol or other drugs. We use drugs to reduce stress, to turn off negative events, to not feel bad. That is one edge of the sword. The other edge is that stress can result from the use of alcohol or other drugs. Problem outcomes related to AOD use cause us stress and anxiety. Everyone in this program can vouch for this: your DWI arrest has most likely been a major cause of stress. We saw in *Session 3* (if you have not had *Session 3*, ask your provider to review it briefly in this session), that the body experiences stress following a period when we are sedated by alcohol. AOD use can produce stress.

Stress is one of the main triggers to relapse and recidivism. Because of this, we will look more deeply into the issue of stress and look at how we can manage our stress responses. We will also look at one of the relatives of stress and depression.

OBJECTIVES OF SESSION

❯ Review the important points about stress we learned in **DWC Education.**

❯ Look at what has caused stress in your life.

❯ Look at ways to manage stress and then practice these.

❯ Look at how stress is related to recidivism and relapse.

❯ Look at depression and how to manage and overcome depression.

LESSON CONTENT AND FOCUS

Remember the key ideas of the cognitive-behavioral approach to change.

❯ Our thoughts about the outside events make us feel stressed or depressed.

❯ We control our stress and emotions that result from stressful events by managing and changing our thinking.

❯ When we change our thoughts, we get a clue as to how we can change our beliefs. Changing beliefs and the attitudes is the key to long-term changes in our thinking and our behavior.

A. LOOK AT YOUR MASTER PROFILE AND MASTER ASSESSMENT PLAN

If you rated yourself high on using alcohol or other drugs to deal with emotional discomfort and psychological problems, you may be dependent on alcohol or other drugs to deal with stress. Update your MAP.

B. CB MAP EXERCISE

❯ Use an event that is stressful.

❯ Go back over the CB MAP and identify thoughts that will lead to a less stressful outcome.

C. KEY IDEAS ABOUT STRESS

1. **What is stress?** Stress is our response to thinking or judging that the demand of an event or situation goes beyond our ability to cope with the situation. **COPING** IS THE KEY WORD.

2. **Stress comes out of mixing (interaction) your inside world with events or situations in your outside world. Here are some of the roots of stress.**

   ▶ Memories of past major negative or difficult experiences such as divorce, loss of loved one, childhood or adult traumas. These are past stress events that are inside us but are set off by ongoing life experiences.
   ▶ Major negative life events such as death of a loved one, divorce, loss of job or major illness.
   ▶ Daily negative or difficult life events such as daily demands of family and work. These are external.
   ▶ Major and minor positive happenings such as a new job, getting married, having a baby or a salary raise.

3. **Stress is based on our mental responses - our automatic thoughts - to these inside or outside events. These are our automatic thoughts.**

   ▶ You **expect** (automatic thought) something bad to happen to you because of the outside events.
   ▶ You **appraise** or judge that the demands of the event go beyond what you see as your ability or resources to meet those demands.
   ▶ You **attribute** or credit the causes of your stress only to outside events and don't see that your control over stress comes from within you.
   ▶ You **decide** that you cannot handle the demands of the outside world.

4. **When stress occurs, we get out of balance.** We call this balance homeostasis. The body works (demands) at regaining balance through coping responses. These are the efforts to control the stress reactions inside of you. They tell us we have stress.

   ▶ **Physical:** Your body becomes upset. You may have a hard time breathing, your heart beats fast, you may get sweaty or feel weak. We hunger for air or oxygen. We may lose control of our breathing. Being in control of our breathing helps us to be in control of our stress response.
   ▶ **Emotional:** These are anger, guilt, depression and feelings of anxiety. These are your efforts to cope with stress. These are uneasy feelings.
   ▶ **Behavioral:** You may drink, go running, go to a movie, gamble, smoke a cigarette, talk with a friend. Often they are positive and help us cope.
   ▶ **Mental:** The first step to managing stress is through our thinking. If our thoughts fail to give us self-control we lose control over body, emotions and behaviors.

Managing stress means that you have to manage all of these responses - body, emotions, behavior, mental.

5. **What are the best signs that show we are stressed?**

- ◗ **Anxiety:** we feel mentally and emotionally anxious, uneasy, fearful. Often we can't pin down why we feel uneasy or anxious. This makes us more anxious. Anxiety often is a result of a lot of negative events that happen over a period of time.

- ◗ **Panic:** we may experience panic or sudden onset of intense fear or anxiety and usually have body symptoms. We may get short of breath, chest feels tight, heart beats fast.

- ◗ **Emotional feelings:** guilty, angry or depressed. These are the emotional stress patterns or syndromes. Have your counselor review the guilt-anger cycle. This cycle is based on these stress syndromes. We will take a close look at anger and violence in the next session. Managing our moods of anger, guilt and depression helps us to manage our anxiety related to our stress.

6. **How does stress and anxiety in your life trigger relapse and recidivism?**

- ◗ Look at *Figure 2,* page 43, the Mental-Behavior Impaired Control Cycle (ICC). How does this ICC explain how stress can lead to relapse and recidivism?

- ◗ This diagram may help you see more clearly how stress can trigger relapse and recidivism. This is what happens to many repeat impaired driving offenders.

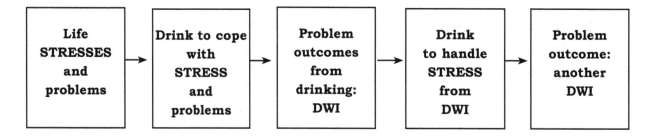

D. LET'S EVALUATE THE ROOTS OR SOURCES OF OUR STRESS

1. **The memory of past major negative events we have experienced. <u>Exercise:</u>** Check if you have had any of these happen to you.

- ❑ Serious childhood illness.
- ❑ Childhood emotional, physical or sexual abuse.
- ❑ Loss of someone close or loved one in childhood.
- ❑ Loss of close family member.

- ❑ Loss of spouse or intimate partner.
- ❑ Divorce or separation from intimate partner.
- ❑ Loss of important job or work position.
- ❑ Making a difficult geographic move.

If you checked several of these, you may have had more than the average amount of stress in your life.

2. **Stressful areas or situations in your life in recent times.**

▶ **Exercise:** Do *Work Sheet 21,* page 87. Answer each question based on the past year. Check whether these were related to your use of alcohol (or other drugs). If your score was *5 to 9,* you may have been experiencing some stress in your life. A score of *10 to 15* means you probably have had moderate stress. A score of *16 or above* indicates that you may have had a high amount of stress in the past year.

▶ **Exercise:** The stress ladder. Do *Work Sheet 22,* page 88. *Work Sheet 21* may not have listed your stress areas or situations. *Work Sheet 22* helps you list the stress areas in your life. Follow the instructions at the top of the *Work Sheet.* Discuss with your group what you found.

E. STEPS FOR COPING WITH AND MANAGING STRESS

Step one: Understanding your stress areas. *Work Sheets 21 and 22,* pages 87 and 88, should give you this information.

Step two: Understand your reactions to stress or symptoms.
Exercise: Do *Work Sheet 23,* page 89. Check those symptoms you have had. List others that you have had that are not on the list. If you checked five or more, you may need some special help in coping with your stress. Talk with your counselor about this.

Step three: What are the typical thoughts that you have to stressful situations? Are these thoughts that magnify, jump to conclusions, catasrophize, blame, make mountains out of mole hills? Are they depressed thoughts, angry thoughts?

Step four: Use the self-control skills to managing stress. You did this in Work *Sheet 22.* We gave them to you in *Session 1.* Here are some to help you manage stress:

▶ *Self-talk.* This is talking to ourselves.

   • Thought stopping.
   • Planting a positive thought.
   • Talking down your emotions.
   • Talking sense to yourself.
   • Arguing against your thought.

▶ *Shifting the view.* Look at the event from a different view. "My kids demand too much from me." Change the view. "My children need me and I have a lot to give to them."

▶ *Go to court with your thoughts.* Fight the errors in thinking that make you anxious.

◗ *Learn to relax.*

- People who relax 15 to 20 minutes a day have fewer illnesses and better physical and mental health.

- Here are just a few tips on how to relax. Do these about 10 or 15 minutes each day.

    ◆ Find a quiet place.

    ◆ Take a few deep breaths and then pay attention to your breathing.

    ◆ Close your eyes and relax your body.

    ◆ Think of a peaceful and calm scene.

    ◆ Relax your muscles by tensing them and relaxing them.

- If your score on *Work Sheet 21* was 10 or more and/or you had more than four or five checks on *Work Sheet 23*, you may want to spend more time learning to relax.

- Therapy Project 4, page 211, will give you some very good ways to learn to relax. Look at those now. You may want to choose this as one of your therapy projects.

Step five: Talk with someone about your stress and anxiety.

Step six: Change your lifestyle and get a better balance. We will look at this in a later session.

Step seven: Evaluate how these steps worked. Always ask yourself: "How am I doing?"

F. DEPRESSION: AN EMOTIONAL STRESS PATTERN

1. Depression is a major emotional stress pattern that can come from stressful events.

   ◗ When depressed, we feel gloom, despair, dejected and deflated. We don't care.

   ◗ You may be using depression to cope with stress.

   ◗ An important part of depression is negative thinking.

2. Depression can be a trigger for both relapse and recidivism.

   ◗ Alcohol or other drugs are often used to cope with depression. Depression can trigger AOD use.

   ◗ SINCE ALCOHOL IS A DEPRESSANT, drinking will most likely make you more depressed. It is depression that comes from drinking. This puts you in the impaired control cycle.

3. Depression can trigger recidivism.

   ◗ Depression can be a trigger for relapse. Relapse is an important step into recidivism.

   ◗ If you are depressed, you are apt to think, "I don't care." If you are depressed and drink, your "I don't care" thinking gets stronger. If you are in a high risk situation for drinking and driving, the "I don't care" thinking puts you at high risk for impaired driving.

4. <u>**Exercise:**</u> **Complete** *Work Sheet 24,* **page 90***,* **Depression Questionnaire (DQ). The higher the score, the more depression you are disclosing. Use these guidelines.**

 ▶ A score in the range of 30 or above suggests that you are in a higher range of depression, and you will most likely want to seek further evaluation and/or help.

 ▶ A score in the range of around 20 to 30 suggests that you are disclosing enough depression that you may want to seek help or at least seek an opinion of a counselor or therapist.

 ▶ A score from around 10 to 20 suggests you are disclosing some depression, but it may be in the low range. You may want to talk it over with a counselor.

 ▶ A score of under 10 would indicate you are probably having a normal amount of depression. If you answered "no" to all or most of the questions, you may be defending against feeling depressed.

5. **Ways to cope with and overcome depression.**

 ▶ **Be aware of your depression.** Understand it. The DQ in *Work Sheet 24* are symptoms of depression. Your score will give you a clue of how much depression you might have.

 ▶ **Change your depressed thoughts** that lead to feelings of depression and depressed behavior.

   • Try to get a handle on those thoughts. Some examples: "I don't care," "I'm worthless," "I'm tired," "Things are hopeless," and "What's the use."

   • Negative thinking is part of depression. Use the mental skills that you learned to manage and change negative thinking.

   • Stress is part of depression. Use the skills above to manage and cope with stress.

   • Keep track of your depressed thoughts. Write them in a notebook. Then, work on changing them.

   • Change your negative and depressed thoughts to positive thoughts.

 ▶ **Understand and change your core beliefs that are beneath your depression.** Some might be: "I'm no good." "I can't be successful." "I'm really not that important."

 ▶ **Know the past and present events and situations that lead to your depression.**

   • Being overwhelmed with so many things to do.

   • Past and present losses.

   • The events and situations that bring on stressful thinking are often the same for depression.

 ▶ **Take action.** Helpless thinking can lead to depression. Take a stand. Take charge of your life. Be in control. Don't react. Act.

 ▶ **Seek professional help for the problem.**

   • Talk with your doctor about medication. Depression can be due to a chemical imbalance. Overcoming your depression may take more than following the steps above.

   • You may decide to enroll in a therapy program for depression.

G. **THE POSITIVE FACES OF ANXIETY, STRESS AND THE EMOTIONS OF DEPRESSION, GUILT AND ANGER**

We often think that anxiety and stress and their emotional expressions of depression, guilt and anger are unhealthy. Not true. All have their positive sides.

- **Anxiety and stress.** Healthy anxiety can spur us to action. Research has shown that some anxiety is necessary for being successful. Anxiety also tells us that something is wrong. When we feel stressed, this is an alarm that should wake us up to the fact that we might be doing too much, taking too much on.

- **Depression is one way that we control our stress.** Sometimes, it is healthy to say, "I don't care what happens. I've done all I can." Healthy depression can help us "not care just enough" to let go, to not always have to be in control, and to get some distance from all of the demands that can overwhelm us.

- **Healthy guilt** helps us to be concerned about how our actions affect others and to CARE. It is an important part of being prosocial.

- **Anger.** We will look at that in our next session.

SESSION AND HOMEWORK ACTIVITIES

A. Update your Master Skills list and ratings, page 31. Are your ratings getting better?

B. **Session Exercise:** One member of the group will be asked to share a stressful situation they are having in their life. After the member shares this situation, the group will be asked to help this person manage the stress by going through each stress management step in E section above, page 83.

C. Chart your AOD thinking and use pattern for this week.

D. Mentally monitor your stress events this week and apply some of the steps we outlined above.

CLOSURE PROCESS GROUP

Share with your group the stresses in your life. Talk about how you handle them.

Here are events or situations that cause stress. Answer these questions as to whether these have been sources of stress for you over the past year. This would include the period before and after your DWI arrest. This is only for your benefit. Put a check in the column that best fits your answer. For each check in the "sometimes" column, give yourself one point; for each check in "A Lot" column, give yourself two points. Then, in the last column, check if your use of alcohol (or other drugs), even on occasion, was a response to these stress events.

WORKSHEET 21

HAVE THESE SITUATIONS IN YOUR LIFE CAUSED YOU STRESS IN THE PAST YEAR?	0 NO	1 SOME-TIMES	2 A LOT	ALCOHOL USE WAS A RESPONSE TO THESE
1. Too many job demands				
2. Demands of family life				
3. Conflict with spouse or partner				
4. Not having a job or work				
5. Keeping up my home/house				
6. Paying my bills/not enough money				
7. Demands from relationships				
8. Your DWI arrest				
9. Your use of alcohol or other drugs				
10. Medical problems or illness				
11. Divorce or separation				
12. Death of a loved one				
TOTAL SCORE				

The stress ladder. List your five most important areas of stress. In the number FIVE space, list the situation or area that is most stressful for you or your highest stress area. Then, in the number ONE space, list the situation or area that is least stressful for you. Then go from space TWO to FOUR and list situations or areas that have increasing levels of stress for you. Then, in column 2, list the methods that you would use to handle those stressful situations or areas.

LIST THE AREAS OR SITUATIONS OF STRESS IN YOUR LIFE NOW	LIST THE SKILLS YOU WOULD USE TO MANAGE THE STRESS
FIVE:	
FOUR:	
THREE:	
TWO:	
ONE:	

Here is a list of responses that people have to stressful situations. Check those that you have had in the past year. List any others that you have had that are not on this list.

WHICH OF THESE REACTIONS HAVE YOU HAD TO STRESSFUL SITUATIONS?	NEVER	SOMETIMES	A LOT
1. Get sweaty, hot			
2. Shortness of breath			
3. Heart beats fast			
4. Feel jumpy, nervous			
5. Stomach gets tense/nervous			
6. Get depressed			
7. Get irritated, angry			
8. Blow things up in my mind			
9. Jump to conclusions			
10. Get all worried and tense			
11. Get a tension headache			
12. Muscles get all tight			
13. Think negative: nothing works			
14. Panic			
15. Drink, use drugs			
16. Other:			
17. Other:			
18. Other:			
19. Other:			
20. Other:			

WORKSHEET 24			

ANSWER AS TO WHETHER THESE APPLY TO YOU AT THIS TIME IN YOUR LIFE	0 NEVER	1 SOMETIMES	2 OFTEN
1. Get tired easily			
2. Sit around and do nothing			
3. Lower sexual drive than usual			
4. Jumpy and quick to react			
5. Hard time doing my work			
6. Loss of appetite and weight			
7. Gained lot of weight			
8. Not sleeping well			
9. Sleeping way too much			
10. Feel like a failure			
11. Have lot of negative thoughts			
12. Lost interest in things			
13. Feeling sad and not happy			
14. Feel disappointed in myself			
15. Hopeless about the future			
16. Cry a lot			
17. Feel like not wanting to live			
18. Can't think clearly			
19. Feel overwhelmed			
20. Feel guilty			

SKILLS IN COGNITIVE SELF-CONTROL

RECOGNIZING AND MANAGING ANGER

OVERVIEW AND SESSION OBJECTIVES

THE FEELING OF ANGER is neither good nor bad, right or wrong. We all have angry feelings from time to time. It is how we act on those feelings, or the actions resulting from the feelings that is right or wrong, good or bad.

When you take part in a behavior that hurts or can potentially hurt other people, **this is often an angry act.** Getting high or drunk often hurts others. It is often an angry act. DWI behavior has the potential of hurting others. Everyone who drives impaired knows this. In fact, **impaired driving often does hurt other people.** In **DWC Education,** you identified those persons who were hurt by your DWI behavior. **Is impaired driving behavior an angry act?** Think about this. Some experts conclude that the DWI is a crime of violence. This may be true, since it kills more than 17,000 persons each year.

OBJECTIVES OF THIS SESSION:

▶ Learn to recognize angry thoughts and feelings.

▶ Understand that anger is usually caused by some problem, and that we need alternatives for successful problem solving.

▶ Become aware of the events that normally trigger anger and of the mental and physical signals you may experience when angry.

▶ Understand the difference between anger, aggression and violence.

▶ Learn the steps of handling anger in a positive way.

START THIS SESSION BY:

▶ Reviewing your work on your AOD Weekly Monitoring Chart.

▶ Doing the CB exercise using an event that led to something that was stressful.

SESSION CONTENT AND FOCUS

WHEN WE GREW UP, often we were not allowed to be angry. If we showed anger, we were told to "cool" it and so we did not learn to express it. Thus, we may not have developed skills to deal with anger. But emotions just don't go away. You can shove them down only so long. If we did not learn healthy outlets for anger and hostility, we built them up inside. When we got high, we could let them go, but in destructive ways. We blew up, were irrational, or hurt others emotionally and even physically. When we came down from the high, and sobered up, we would recall what we said and did. We didn't feel good about our actions and may have had strong thoughts and feelings of guilt. This again kept us from dealing with our anger.

A. YOUR MASTER PROFILE MAY INDICATE YOU HAVE SPECIAL NEEDS OF MANAGING ANGER AND EMOTIONAL DISTRESS

▶ You probably have special needs in the area of *anger management* if you have high self-ratings on AOD use to cope with emotional discomfort, problems with the law, behavioral disruption from use, and the thinking assessment items relating to anger. Did you account for these problems in your *Master Assessment Plan?*

▶ Anger is a threat to your self-control. It is a big trigger to relapse and recidivism. This session is about managing and controlling anger so as to have positive outcomes.

B. WHAT ARE THE CLUES AND SIGNS OF ANGER?

▶ *Your body and physical signs:*
- tense muscles;
- shakiness and trembling;
- getting red in the face; and
- sweating, rapid breathing, fast heart beat.

▶ *What you say to yourself - your thoughts:*
- thoughts of being "short-changed,;
- not being treated fairly;
- thinking that you're a victim;
- thinking, "it's not fair;"
- "they deserve it;"
- thinking that your personal space is being violated, feel being pushed by someone.

▶ *How you feel:*
- agitated and irritable;
- feelings are hurt;
- humiliated and insulted;
- tense, on edge;
- impatient, things not going your way;
- feeling out of control.

▶ *Your actions:*
- fly off the handle;
- restless;
- quick body motions; and
- lose temper.

Remember: events do not cause anger. It is the *thoughts* and underlying beliefs that we have about those the events that lead to anger. Often, the outside events are usually some problem or a situation that can be resolved. Thoughts that lead to anger are often caused by some problem situation. These are high-charged situations. These are situations that bring angry thoughts. We can control much of our anger by controlling these thoughts.

C. TWO KINDS OF EXTERNAL EVENTS THAT LEAD TO ANGRY THINKING AND MAY BE HIGH-CHARGED SITUATIONS

▶ *Relationship conflicts* and problems are usually based on not being understood, feeling powerless, not feeling approved of, perception of having needs blocked and not getting what you want from the other person.

▶ *Non-interpersonal* event or problem situation such as being stuck in traffic, losing your billfold, breaking a favorite object.

Remember, it's **your thoughts** that produce your emotions. Angry thoughts lead to angry feelings and actions. *Anger is not caused by events, but by your thoughts in response to those events.*

D. ANGER, HOSTILITY, AGGRESSION AND VIOLENCE

1. **Anger is an emotion or a feeling - aggression is a behavior.** When anger is directed toward the goal of harming or injuring another living being, then it is aggression. Aggression is attacking, controlling and provoking. Aggression may be non-physical or physical.

   ▶ *Non-physical aggression* is verbal and non-verbal behavior that abuses, injures or hurts someone emotionally or psychologically.

   - It can damage another person's sense of dignity and self.
   - It can lower another person's self-esteem.
   - It can be directed at a person's sexual well-being.
   - It can damage a person emotionally, creating lasting emotional injury, e.g., fear, anxiety, depression, hostility and anger.
   - It can cause a person to withdraw from others and feel threatened.
   - It can be calculated or impulsive.
   - It can be controlled or it can be uncontrolled rage.

   ▶ *Failure to control your anger* can lead to aggressive behavior. It is a threat to your freedom. It's all about self-control. This is one of the most important skills for you to learn. Your success will depend on self-control. **Self-control leads to positive outcomes.**

2. **Hostility** is an underlying attitude that gets expressed when we *appraise* or judge others as acting towards us in harmful ways. It is often seen as a personality trait.

   ◗ Hostility is a way of orienting yourself to the outside world - *attitude*.
   ◗ Whereas anger and violence are triggered by outside events, hostility comes from within.
   ◗ Hostility can feed the anger response or violence.

3. **Violence occurs when aggression becomes physical.** Physical aggression is VIOLENCE: Violence does everything that non-physical aggression does, but it involves being physical. It causes physical harm and damage to things and people.

   ◗ Violence can be directed towards objects involving smashing and breaking things but this violence is always person oriented; it is always about someone.
   ◗ Violence can be directed at a person and can focus on the other person's:

     • *position of strength or power* - this is when the victim has the strength or power to get in the way of the violent person's needs or goals and the violent person is initially weak;
     • *position of weakness* - this is when the victim is weak and the violent person has to maintain a position of strength; and
     • *position of sex* - this is when the victim is a target of the violent person's distorted sexual drives.

   ◗ Sooner or later, non-physical aggression will end up in violence unless the aggression is controlled and dealt with in a positive manner.
   ◗ How do you see your own history of aggression and violence?

   Exercise: Share your views of this in group.

E. GETTING ANGRY INVOLVES THREE STEPS

   ◗ You experience stress and frustration.
   ◗ You blame someone for your situation - blame is the basis of much of our anger. You find someone else responsible for your misery or distress.
   ◗ You direct your emotion or distress - now called anger - towards someone or something.

F . HERE ARE THE BASIC APPROACHES OR STEPS TO MANAGING AND CONTROLLING ANGER AND AGGRESSIVE IMPULSES AND PREVENTING VIOLENCE

1. **Be aware of your anger.**

   ◗ *Be aware* of your anger when you feel it. *Use self-talk.* Say to yourself "I'm angry."

▶ *Try to identify* what you are stressed about.

▶ *Be aware* of what you are angry about. What are your angry thoughts?

Exercise: Use *Work Sheet 25*, page 99, to list some of the things or situations that you have been angry about. Then, list the angry thoughts you had about those situations.

▶ *Pay attention* to what goes on inside you when you get angry. You may feel your stomach churn, increased sweating, clenched fists, tight muscles, or any number of other sensations.

▶ *Recognize* that you are blaming someone or something.

2. **Know what triggers your anger.**

▶ *Most people have specific triggers that lead to angry thoughts such as an attack on you or someone keeping you from reaching your goal or being blamed or accused.*

▶ *Exercise: Group members will be asked to share their triggers.*

3. **Know the difference between feeling angry and the results of being angry.** *Being angry might include aggression and violence.* Anger is a powerful feeling. It is not good or bad. It is how we show or act out our anger that makes the difference. It can be destructive or constructive.

4. **Ask, "Is my anger destructive or constructive anger"?**

▶ **Destructive anger** confuses people and leads to bad outcomes. It makes people aggressive and mad at us. This blocks communication. It leaves us feeling helpless. It knocks down feelings of self-worth.

▶ **Constructive anger** expresses the emotions in such a way that you feel better afterwards but it builds communication. People know you are angry and they listen. It can trigger problem solving. It helps you to be *assertive.*

5. **Use self-control techniques right away when you feel the anger build**. Without *self-control,* you can't express your anger in constructive ways. You just get angry. These skills will help.

▶ Use *self-talk.* "CALM DOWN AND STAY COOL." Hear your own voice calm yourself. Hear the angry thought. Use thought stopping and coping statements.

▶ Use *relaxation skills.* Take five deep breaths and exhale slowly, counting to ten, or counting backward from 20, leaving the situation.

▶ **Think** about the negative or bad outcomes that can come from uncontrolled anger.

▶ Use *thought replacement.* **Replace the angry thoughts with positive thoughts.** Remember in *Session 6* you learned how to *arm yourself with positive thoughts.* Look at your list. Use one of those.

▶ **Exercise:** construct the anger ladder using *Worksheet 26*, page 100. We will use this ladder later.

6. **Express or communicate your anger.** Don't just get angry. Tell people you are angry. Don't act it out. Use the "I" message. "I'm feeling angry. I'm mad." You act out your anger when you **blame** others, when you use the "you message," when you yell and when you turn against someone physically.

   ▶ A healthy expression of anger is not "blowing up" or just getting it off your chest.

   ▶ Express your anger to communicate the thoughts that bring on the anger. If you yell, you don't communicate thoughts. They can't hear what you think. Make your expression of anger win-win, think, "How can we both learn from this."

   ▶ Take responsibility for your anger. When you express it, think "It's my anger. I own it. It's not someone else's fault."

   ▶ It is a falsehood that you have to get angry in order to not let it build up. When you talk about your anger, it doesn't build up.

   ▶ Research is clear: getting angry just to "feel better" or get it "off my chest" does not solve the problem behind the anger.

7. **After you communicate or express your anger**

   ▶ Again ask yourself "What am I angry about?" Was it rational? Did it make sense?

   ▶ *Let the other person respond.* The other person may also be angry and not reasoning well. This may put you in harm's way.

8. **Study your anger and your angry thoughts after you have expressed your anger and you're over it.** What am I really angry about? What were my thoughts? What are the positive things about this situation? Try to understand exactly what happened.

9. **Start problem solving even when you feel the anger build and when you are expressing your anger.** Anger is usually about some problem - conflict with another person, losing something.

   ▶ What are my angry thoughts?
   ▶ What am I angry about?
   ▶ What is the problem that is bringing the thoughts?

     • What is my goal?
     • Choose an action! This action should replace the angry thoughts.

   ▶ The goal is not just to feel better. It is to manage the anger while you are solving the problem that brings on the angry thoughts.

We will study problem solving later in this program.

10. If you are successful, be proud and congratulate yourself. Reward yourself.

LEARN TO EXPRESS YOUR ANGRY THOUGHTS, NOT JUST YOUR ANGRY FEELINGS. YOU'RE SO ANGRY I CAN'T HEAR YOUR THOUGHTS. SELF-CONTROL IS THE KEY.

G. PRACTICE SELF-CONTROL

1. **With the help of your counselor and group, start with the number one situation on your anger ladder,** *Worksheet 26.* Imagine that scene. Now practice these relaxation techniques.

   ‣ Relax by taking slow, deep breaths.
   ‣ Inhale slowly, hold your breath, count to two and then release your breath.
   ‣ Repeat your deep breathing exercise, releasing your breath slowly.
   ‣ Now clear your mind of all thoughts, and if a thought interrupts, tell yourself, "I AM RELAXED." REPEAT THIS EXERCISE.

2. **Take the number two scene on the anger ladder.** This time use self-talk to address the feelings of anger and to develop control over the anger. Use thought stopping to do this. Go through the steps outlined above to manage and control your anger. Work up the ladder.

3. **Make sure you have worked through any angry feelings that come out of this session.** If you still have some leftover anger, talk to the group or your counselor.

SELF-CONTROL LEADS TO POSITIVE OUTCOMES. SELF-CONTROL COMES THROUGH BEING IN CHARGE OF OUR THOUGHTS.

SESSION AND HOMEWORK ACTIVITIES

A. Update your Master Skills list, page 31. Add a date to the anger management skills item.

B. **HOMEWORK:** Use *Work Sheet 27* and do a Thinking Report on self-control. Take an event that happens to you this coming week in which you become angry but manage to control the emotion.

C. Do your AOD Weekly Monitoring Chart for next week.

CLOSURE PROCESS GROUP

Openly share how you see your problems, if any, with anger in your life.

Looking at your anger and angry thoughts. List some situations that you have been angry about. Then write down the angry thoughts you had about those situations.

LIST SITUATIONS YOU WERE ANGRY ABOUT	LIST YOUR ANGRY THOUGHTS

The anger ladder. List high charged situations that can lead you to anger or aggression. In the number FIVE space, list the situation that would make you the most angry. In the number ONE space, list the situation that would make you the least angry. Then go from space TWO to FOUR and list situations that have increasing levels of anger for you. In column 2, list the methods that you would use to handle your anger in those situations.

LIST HIGH-CHARGED SITUATIONS THAT HAVE LED TO YOUR GETTING ANGRY, HAVING ANGRY THOUGHTS AND EVEN FEELINGS OF AGGRESSION	LIST THE METHODS YOU WOULD USE TO MANAGE THE SITUATION OR YOUR ANGER
FIVE:	
FOUR:	
THREE:	
TWO:	
ONE:	

WORKSHEET 27

Thinking report: Use an event that happened to you this week in which you became angry but did control the emotion

THINKING REPORT
DESCRIBE THE EVENT:
YOUR THOUGHTS:
YOUR FEELINGS:
YOUR ATTITUDES AND BELIEFS:
THE OUTCOME:

SESSION 10

SOCIAL AND RELATIONSHIP SKILLS BUILDING

LEARNING COMMUNICATION TOOLS AND SKILLS

INTRODUCTION AND SESSION OBJECTIVES

THIS IS ONE OF FOUR sessions that focuses on improving and building social and relationship skills. An important part of these sessions will involve sharing information about yourself and getting feedback from others. Self-awareness is a key to opening the door to change our thinking, feelings and actions. There are two pathways to self-awareness. One is through *self-disclosure* - sharing our personal experiences and problems. The other is to have others give us *feedback* - having others tell us what they see and feel about what we have shared and disclosed. In this session, we will work on communication skills for self-disclosure.

Communication is always a two way process. It involves talking about ourselves **and** getting others to talk and share about themselves. Thus, we will also develop skills to help others disclose to us and to learn skills to give feedback to others. This is a new step in this program. Up to now, we have focused mainly on self-disclosing and receiving feedback from others.

The purpose of this session is to *learn basic communication skills* and to apply these skills to strengthen responsible living.

OBJECTIVES OF THIS SESSION

▪ Understand verbal and nonverbal communication.
▪ Learn and practice the basic skills of self-oriented communication - **active sharing,** which is self-disclosure and receiving feedback from others.
▪ Learn and practice the basic skills of other-directed communication - **active listening** or getting others to talk to you, to have others be open to receiving feedback from you.

There is power in what we are about to learn and practice. It is the power of communication. It is the power of talking and the power of listening.

START THE GROUP BY:

▪ Reviewing the thinking report you did this week - *Worksheet 27,* page 100, and
▪ Doing the CB MAP Exercise.

SESSION CONTENT AND FOCUS

A. TWO KINDS OF COMMUNICATION WE USE IN RELATING TO OTHERS: NON-VERBAL AND VERBAL

1. **Non-verbal communication is "talking" without words.** We tell others how we think and feel through our face, how we move our body and in the tone of our voice. What we show by our talking without words (nonverbal communication) often is not the same as our talking with words (verbal communication). If we are to have people understand us, we must say the same thing with words that we say without words.

Here are some different way that we express ourselves or "talk" without words or non-verbally.

- Our posture.
- Space between us and the other person.
- Eye contact.
- Facial expressions.
- Head nods.
- Tone of voice.
- Silence.

Exercise: Show the following emotions without words. What are your thoughts when you show these emotions non-verbally?

ANGER FEAR SHAME JOY LOVE SURPRISE

Exercise: Practice making your non-verbal message match your verbal message by role playing the following:

- Telling someone you are angry with him/her;
- Telling someone you like them;
- Telling someone you love them.

2. **Verbal communication is talking with words.** When using words to communicate, we need to check out if the other person is understanding us. Keep in mind that people have different opinions. Those opinions are based on how each of us sees the world. Most often, these opinions are not right or wrong. Clear and honest verbal communication helps other people understand us and helps us better understand our own thoughts, feelings and behaviors. Then we can change those thoughts and behaviors that are hurting us and others.

OPINIONS are different from FACTS. We can solve problems if we stick to the facts **and** hear the opinion of others. Sometimes the same words have different meanings like "fly," or "light." Sometimes different words have the same meaning, like "young man," "boy," "lad." Opinions can have different meanings - that's why it is sometimes hard to communicate clearly.

Exercise: Have each member of your group give their meaning to the words "fly," and "light."

B. TWO PATHWAYS TO COMMUNICATION: SELF-ORIENTED COMMUNICATION AND OTHER-ORIENTED COMMUNICATION

There are two ways that we direct ourselves in communicating with others: *self-oriented communication* and *other-oriented communication.* Both are important if you want to understand and be understood. Both are basic to positive and successful relationships with others. Both are necessary for responsible living.

1. **Active sharing or self-oriented communication.** This is communication about you. There are two skills that make for successful active sharing - self-disclosure and receiving feedback.

   a. **Self-disclosure** or **telling the other person about you** involves talking about yourself and not the other person. It is sharing with someone - your counselor, your group - how you see your past and your current feelings, thoughts and actions.

   ▶ It is using the "I" message in communication. There are four basic parts to this communication.

      • I think.
      • I feel.
      • I need.
      • I do or I act.

   ▶ The most *unselfish* thing you can do is to **start a sentence off with "I."** Why? Because when you use the word "I," *you share yourself.* Sharing yourself is unselfish. Active sharing is about you, not about the other person. It's not bragging. I'ts just being honest about you. Most important, you hear yourself through you.

   ▶ Self-disclosure does three things. These are keys to change.

      • It tells you about yourself. It is you talking to yourself. You are disclosing to yourself and making yourself more aware.
      • It allows others to see who you are and allows others to give you honest feedback on how they see you.
      • It helps others to self-disclose to you.

   ▶ *Use the word "I" and not "you" in this kind of communication.* When we start with the word "you," we are talking about the other person, and not about our own feelings and thoughts. When we are mad at someone, or in conflict, we use the word "you." We want to blame, tell the other person what he or she should do or did. Practice talking with others using only the word "I" and not the word "you."

▶ Active sharing may involve telling another person that you are upset or bothered by that person's actions. Here are some tips on how to have this result in a positive outcome.

- Use "I" messages. Avoid "you" messages or blaming statements.
- Use self-talk to stay in control and be calm. "I need to be calm."
- Focus on the person's actions or specific behavior and not on the person himself/herself.
- Be firm, clear and specific.
- Make it clear it is about you, what is acceptable to you. That it is their choice to act this way, but your choice is to allow yourself to be exposed to those actions.
- Bring closure to your statements. Don't go on and on. Finish on a positive note. "I appreciate your listening to me."
- Give the other person a chance to share his or her thoughts and feelings. Listen to what the other person has to say.

Exercise: Role play telling someone in your life you are upset with them. Have someone in the group be that person. Use the above tips. Make the outcome positive. Do not use the word "you." Use only "I" messages.

b. **Listening to feedback from others about you** is the second key skill to active sharing.

▶ You hear yourself through others. This is hard to do. When people talk to you **about you** - it should be because you give them permission.

▶ The key to receiving feedback is to **not get defensive.** When we get defensive, we stop that person from giving us feedback. If the feedback is critical or negative, we often get openly defensive. When feelings and emotions are high between two people, this is not always possible. *The feedback becomes blaming.* If you want feedback, try *not to get defensive.* Sometimes we even push away feedback that is a compliment or positive. We will look at the skill of receiving compliments in a later session.

▶ Feedback is less threatening if the other person makes it clear that this is only his or her opinion, and is not necessarily true. What you really say is "Tell me about me." We will look at what makes up good feedback statements as we look at other-oriented communication below.

Figure 8, page 106, provides a picture of self-oriented communication or active sharing.

Exercise: Using only a few words, share with the group how you think you are doing in the program. Then one person in the group will give you feedback as to how he or she thinks you are doing.

Exercise: Go over *Worksheet 28,* page 109, your active sharing homework for this week.

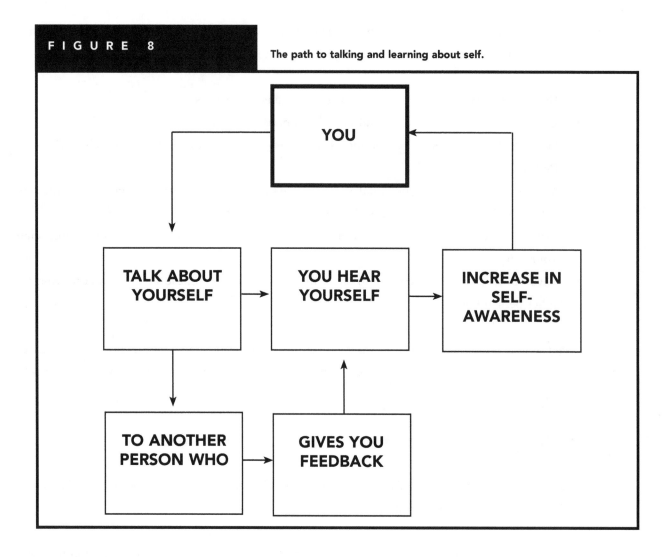

FIGURE 8   The path to talking and learning about self.

YOU

TALK ABOUT YOURSELF

YOU HEAR YOURSELF

INCREASE IN SELF-AWARENESS

TO ANOTHER PERSON WHO

GIVES YOU FEEDBACK

2. **Active listening or other-orienting communication is getting people to talk to you and you share how you see them.**

▶   There are two skills in other-directed communication or active listening.

     a.   **Inviting others to share** by using the open statement and open question skills.

         •   This encourages people to tell you about them. "Tell me how you feel." "How are you doing today?"

         •   Avoid "Do you?" questions. Those are closed questions. Closed statements get a "yes" or "no" answer.

     b.   **Giving feedback or reflective listening.** "This is how I see you," or "I see you are upset." We call these reflective listening or active listening skills.

▶ Bypass your "thinking filters": Choosing an "open channel" to listen.

- Our "thinking filters" are the screens that we run through what other people say.
- These thinking filters are our beliefs, our attitudes and our values. We don't have to give up these beliefs and attitudes to listen.
- When we have an open listening channel, our response comes from that channel and not our "thinking filters."
- When we run what we see and hear through our "thinking filter," we may twist and distort what we are hearing.

▶ Listen and watch for the non-verbal behavior. "Listen" to body talk or body language. Some body talk that we can listen to and learn from are:

- posture;
- facial expressions;
- voice tone;
- personal space; and
- hand, face and feet gestures.

▶ **Here are some points for good active listening.**

- Look at the person you are talking with. *Establish comfortable eye contact.*
- Let the other person finish what they are saying.
- Watch the person's *body language.*
- *Pay attention* to what is being said. If you don't understand, ask an open question or make an open statement, such as, "Tell me more."
- Show interest in what the other person is saying.
- When you do understand, *nod your head* to encourage the speaker.
- Reflect back what you hear; mirror back what you hear. This tells the other person you hear them.
- Use some ACTIVE SHARING skills. Share with the other person what you think and feel.

▶ **Active listening helps us to:**

- build positive relationships;
- connects us with others so we aren't lonely;
- shows respect for others;
- makes life more interesting.

▶ **Exercise:** Go over *Work Sheet 29,* page 109, your active listening homework.

C. PRACTICING ACTIVE SHARING AND ACTIVE LISTENING

Exercise: Break up into groups of three. Have one person use active sharing or "I" messages. The second person listens using active listening skills. The third person watches and gives feedback on how well the other two are doing. Then change roles. PRACTICE...PRACTICE...PRACTICE.

Exercise: Role play a situation where one person is telling another person a problem he/she is having communicating with his/her spouse. How did they do on the skills of active listening and active sharing?

SESSION ACTIVITIES AND HOMEWORK

A. Update your Master Skills list and ratings, page 31. Are your ratings getting higher?

B. **TRY TO USE ONLY "I" MESSAGES FOR THE COMING WEEK.** Did you find yourself talking about the other person, and not about your feelings and thoughts about the other person? Did you use "you" messages more than the "I" messages?

C. Do *Work Sheets 28* and *29, Homework for Active Listening* and *Homework for Active Sharing.*

D. For homework, using *Work Sheet 30,* page 110, do a thinking report on a time when you got defensive during the week. Then, in the NOTES at the bottom of *Work Sheet 30,* write down the number of times you defended yourself this week. How could you have made it better by using the communication skills above?

E. Do your AOD Weekly Monitoring Chart.

CLOSURE PROCESS GROUP

Discuss how you get defensive with people close to you. Talk about the last time you got defensive.

Active sharing. Take one situation when you were practicing active sharing this week.

1. DESCRIBE THE SITUATION:

2. WHO WAS INVOLVED?

3. WHAT SPECIFIC ACTIVE SHARING SKILLS DID YOU USE?

4. HOW DID THEY WORK? DID THE OTHER PERSON LISTEN? DID YOU RECEIVE FEEDBACK? DID YOU GET DEFENSIVE?

Active listening. Take one situation where you were practicing active listening this week.

1. DESCRIBE THE SITUATION:

2. WHO WAS INVOLVED?

3. WHAT SPECIFIC ACTIVE LISTENING SKILLS DID YOU USE?

4. HOW DID THEY WORK? DID THE OTHER PERSON LISTEN? DID YOU GIVE FEEDBACK? DID THE OTHER PERSON GET DEFENSIVE?

WORKSHEET 30

1. DESCRIBE THE EVENT:

2. YOUR THOUGHTS:

3. YOUR FEELINGS:

4. YOUR ATTITUDES AND BELIEFS:

5. THE OUTCOME:

NOTES: NUMBER OF TIMES I GOT DEFENSIVE THIS WEEK.

SESSION 11

SOCIAL AND RELATIONSHIP SKILLS BUILDING

STARTING AND KEEPING A CONVERSATION GOING

OVERVIEW AND SESSION OBJECTIVES

THIS SESSION builds on the basic communication skills of *active listening* and *active sharing.* We use these basic skills to learn and practice *social* and *interpersonal* coping skills.

For some people, starting a conversation and keeping it going is difficult. Yet, it is a basic communication skill in communicating with others, meeting new people, buying a car, getting a job. Sometimes people find themselves lonely and isolated because they do not feel confident relating to others. Often, this is due to shyness or a reluctance to start talking with someone. This is one reason for drinking - to loosen up enough to talk. People who are shy or who have negative feelings about themselves do not feel comfortable in a social situation without a drink.

Most people can chit-chat, "shoot the breeze." But **starting and maintaining a difficult conversation** may be hard. We tend to avoid conflict and dealing with sensitive issues with people. We may even need a few drinks to approach a person with a topic that is difficult to talk about. You can easily start a conversation with your spouse about going to the store to get groceries. But telling him you are upset because he got home late is another matter. It is not difficult to talk with your neighbor about the weather, but it is not easy to confront him about his barking dog. This session is **also** about **starting a difficult conversation and bringing it to a positive outcome.**

OBJECTIVES OF THIS SESSION

▶ Briefly review the skills of active sharing and active listening.

▶ Learn and practice the skill of starting and keeping a conversation going with the goal of learning to start a difficult conversation and bringing it to a positive outcome.

START THIS SESSION BY:

▶ Reviewing the homework you did on active sharing and active listening, *Worksheet 28* and *29.*

▶ Doing the CB MAP Exercise.

▶ Reviewing the thinking report you did on getting defensive, *Worksheet 30.*

SESSION CONTENT AND FOCUS

A. WHEN STARTING A CONVERSATION, WE USE THE BASIC COMMUNICATION SKILLS WE LEARNED LAST SESSION

1. **Active sharing:** involves the skills of self-disclosure and receiving feedback.

2. **Active listening:** involves using open statements/questions, and using feedback or reflective statements.

B. BASIC GUIDELINES FOR STARTING AND KEEPING A CONVERSATION GOING

▶ You don't have to have an "important" topic. Small talk is OK. Make conversation fun.

▶ Use active listening. You don't have to do all the talking. Encourage the other person to talk about him/herself. When you are finished, do you know something about the other person?

▶ Talk about yourself. Use "I" messages. When you are finished, does the other person know something about you?

▶ Listen to and observe the other person. Is the person open to talking? Is the person in the middle of something?

▶ What is of interest to the other person? Tune into that interest.

▶ Speak clearly and loud enough. Some people have a hard time hearing.

▶ Use open-ended questions and open statements.

- Open statement: "Tell me about what you did."

- Open question: "How are you feeling today?"

▶ Use active listening skills. State what you hear the other person say.

▶ Learn to tell stories. Practice storytelling. It's simple. Just tell someone what happened to you on the way to work. Talk about people you saw during the day.

▶ Conversations should be enjoyable.

▶ END THE CONVERSATION ON A POSITIVE NOTE. Tell the person you enjoyed the talk. Be graceful if you end the conversation. "I have to go now, but it was nice talking with you."

C. STARTING AND MAINTAINING A CONVERSATION AROUND A DIFFICULT OR SENSITIVE TOPIC

▶ This requires more skillful use of active sharing and active listening.

▶ Here are the important steps.
- *First,* **approach** the person when you have time. Don't sandwich it in between TV programs. If it is important, then give it the time it needs.

- *Second,* **set the stage.** Tell the person "I need to talk with you and need some of your time." Tell the person it is important to you.

- *Third,* **negotiate the time, setting and terms.** Is this just a sharing time? Or, do you want to solve a problem? After you state your need, give the other person opportunity to be part of the decision of when and how. The other person may not want to problem solve, but only state a position.

- *Fourth,* **keep the focus on you,** not the other person. Share with the person what you have to say. Make the agenda yours, not the other person's. Use "I" messages. Avoid "you" statements. If you blame, it will only make the other person defensive and not listen. If your goal is to get the other person to listen, then don't talk about them, talk about yourself.

- *Fifth,* **keep to the point and give closure on** what you wanted to talk about. Don't go on and on.

- *Sixth,* **give the other person a chance** to state his or her position and respond. Use *active listening* skills during this step.

- *Seventh,* **bring closure to the sharing phase** or the stating of your position and converse back and fourth. Continue to use "I" messages.

- *Eighth,* **make a decision** between the two of you if you want to move to some problem solving discussion or conversation. It is probably best to keep that for another time if you did not agree to this to begin with.

- *Ninth,* **be satisfied** with having made your statement and conversing about it.

- *Tenth,* **end the conversation on a positive note** even though the problem may not be solved. The fact that you talked may be the positive outcome.

▶ Set the terms of the difficult conversation early on. Problem-solving or entering into decision-making moves the conversation to another stage. In our next session, we will look at the skill of problem solving.

D. PRACTICE THESE SKILLS IN YOUR SESSION

Exercise: Break into pairs and practice starting a conversation. Use the skills learned above. Remember who, where, what you shared, how the other person responded, and the verbal and non-verbal communications used.

Exercise: Share with the group a difficult or sensitive conversation you would like to have with someone important in your life. You may be asked to role play in group.

Exercise: Use *Work Sheet 31,* page 115. Describe a conversation you started in the past couple of weeks that was around a sensitive and difficult topic and that did not turn out well. Share your findings with your group.

SESSION ACTIVITIES AND HOMEWORK

A. Update your Master Skills List and Master Skills ratings, page 31.

B. Do Work Sheet 31, page 115.

C. Do your AOD Weekly Monitoring Chart

CLOSURE PROCESS GROUP

Share your work on your AOD monitoring chart, then share a difficult or sensitive conversation you would like to have with someone close to you.

W O R K S H E E T   3 1

DESCRIBE A DIFFICULT TOPIC CONVERSATION YOU STARTED THAT HAD A BAD OUTCOME	HOW WOULD YOU DO IT DIFFERENTLY, USING THE SKILLS YOU HAVE LEARNED TO GET A GOOD OUTCOME?
Describe the situation and who with:	Describe the situation and who with:
What did you say to start the conversation?	How would you start the conversation now?
What was the other person's response?	Given your different approach, how do you think the other person would now respond?
What was the outcome?	What would the outcome be now?

S E S S I O N 1 2

SOCIAL AND RELATIONSHIP

SKILLS BUILDING

GIVING AND RECEIVING POSITIVE

REINFORCEMENT - PRAISE

OVERVIEW AND SESSION OBJECTIVES

HEALTHY RELATIONSHIPS involve *giving* and *receiving* positive reinforcements. We do this by giving and receiving compliments and praise. Successful relationships depend on this give-and-take where positive experiences are shared and strengthened. Our chances of *receiving in a relationship* are increased *when we give* in that relationship. Our chances of giving in a relationship are increased when we receive from that relationship.

Often, we fail to share the good things we think about our friends, acquaintances and family members. We may assume that they just know we like them or care about them and it isn't neccessary to tell them this. On the other hand, we may have no problem telling other people how much we appreciate them, but may not be able to graciously accept positive reinforcement or compliments.

In a relationship that may have been damaged by DWI conduct and substance abuse, the good things in the friendship or union may get lost. Learning to express appreciation for the good times, the kind responses, the positive moments, is one way to heal a damaged relationship. On the other hand, people who have had AOD use problems or a DWI offense will often have *negative thoughts and feelings* about themselves. They will find it difficult to accept positive reinforcement and support.

OBJECTIVES OF THIS SESSION
▶ Learn the skills involved in giving positive support and sincere compliments and praise.
▶ Learn to accept positive support and compliments from others.

START THIS SESSION BY:

▶ Reviewing your work on your AOD Weekly Monitoring Chart;
▶ Do the CB MAP Exercise, making the event discussing a difficult topic with another person.
▶ Reviewing the skills of **active sharing** and **active listening;** and
▶ Update your MAP.

SESSION CONTENT AND FOCUS

FEELING GOOD about yourself and about how others feel about you are important as you develop the thoughts and actions that lead to self-control and responsible living. One way that we can feel good about ourselves and others is to give and receive positive reinforcement. Here are two specific ways of doing this.

▶ Giving sincere compliments and praise to others.
▶ Learning to accept praise and compliments from others.

A. THERE IS A DIFFERENCE BETWEEN POSITIVE REINFORCEMENT OR PRAISE (COMPLIMENTS) AND THANKS OR APPRECIATION

▶ Thanking someone or *giving gratitude* is usually in response to something that someone has done for you. It is a response that has a clear stimulus - something someone did for you. Although it is almost second nature to people, some people do need to learn the skill of saying "thank you." A "thank you" will focus on the object or favor or what was done for you.

▶ Giving *positive reinforcement,* praise or compliments are not necessarily a response to something someone did for you. You have to attend to other people, observe their behaviors for opportunities to praise. This is why it is difficult to do this at times. Positive reinforcements such as praise and compliments, focus on the thinking, feelings and actions of the other person, not necessarily what was done for you.

This session will focus mainly on the praise or compliment aspect of communication. However, the *skill* of giving praise or positive reinforcement is similar to that of giving thanks or gratitude.

B. GIVING COMPLIMENTS AND PRAISE IS BASED ON OTHER-DIRECTED COMMUNICATION OR ACTIVE LISTENING

Compliments are effective when you know about the other person. We get to know the other person when we use **open statements** and **open questions.** The actual giving of a compliment involves using the **reflection skill.** A compliment is reflecting back what you see as positive about the other person. "I see you are doing a really great job." "You really came through this time." Here are some guidelines for giving praise and compliments.

▶ Make the compliment or reinforcement sincere and real.

▶ What is the point you want to recognize?

▶ Be brief with your praise.

▶ Be specific. What is the action you want to compliment or reinforce? Rather than saying "You're a good guy," say why you think the person is a "good guy." "It was good of you to give me a ride home."

▶ State the compliment or praise both in terms of your thoughts and feelings. "You did a **good job** fixing the door. I **felt proud** of you." This helps the other person feel that the compliment is sincere and really comes from you and not from them. People don't like to compliment themselves.

▶ Be sensitive to the other person's personality when you give compliments and praise. Some people get embarrassed if they are praised or complimented with others around. Give praise to someone who is shy when no one is around.

▶ Listen to the person's response to your praise.

C. RECEIVING COMPLIMENTS IS BASED ON THE SECOND KEY SKILL OF SELF-DIRECTED COMMUNICATION - BEING OPEN AND LISTENING TO FEEDBACK FROM OTHERS ABOUT YOU

▶ Sometimes we may shut down feedback we get from others when we get defensive. We may do this when we receive positive reinforcement or praise. Maybe the compliment is embarrassing.

▶ Receiving a compliment requires that we take ownership of our positive behaviors. This will mean that we also have to take responsibility for our negative behaviors. To own a compliment means that we may have to take ownership of a criticism or correction of our behavior.

▶ We may push away a compliment because we don't think a lot of ourselves. If we have poor self-esteem, we will push away compliments.

▶ Here are some tips on receiving compliments.

- Take time to listen to the praise.
- Do not deny the praise. Be gracious. Let them know it makes you feel good.
- Use clear words to respond back to the praise.
- Even though you may not agree, let them know you like what they said and that you appreciate it.

▶ For these reasons, most people find that it is more difficult to receive a compliment than to give one.

Exercise: *Practice giving and receiving* praise and compliments. Which is easier, giving or receiving the compliment? You may be asked to role play giving and receiving compliments with someone close to you in your life.

SESSION ACTIVITIES AND HOMEWORK

A. Update your Master Skills list, page 31. Review your ratings.

B. **Exercise:** Your counselor will carefully go over Work Sheets 32 and 33, your homework for this week.

C. Focus on giving and receiving compliments during this coming week.

D. Using *Work Sheet 34*, do a thinking report on a situation where you had a chance to compliment someone and you didn't. Then do a rethinking report so that the outcome results in giving a compliment.

E. Do your *AOD Weekly Monitoring Chart* for this coming week.

CLOSURE PROCESS GROUP

Talk about giving and receiving compliments in your group. What are the risks? What are the payoffs? Share some personal experiences in this area.

THINK OF A CLOSE FRIEND OR FAMILY MEMBER WHO MAY NOT KNOW HOW MUCH YOU APPRECIATE HER/HIM. BEFORE THE NEXT GROUP MEETING, MAKE A POINT OF GIVING A POSITIVE REINFORCEMENT OR COMPLIMENTING THAT PERSON.

Describe what happened.

What kind of a compliment did you give?

Were you specific about what you told him/her?

Did you state the compliment in terms of your own thoughts and feelings?

How did the person receive the compliment?

What did you think and feel about praising or complimenting someone?

Practice receiving compliments: Practice receiving compliments or praise this coming week and then write down what happened.

PAY ATTENTION THIS WEEK TO WORDS OF PRAISE OR A COMPLIMENT THAT SOMEONE GAVE YOU. THEN USE THE FOLLOWING POINTS TO SEE HOW YOU HANDLED IT.

What was the compliment or praise the person gave you?

What was your specific action the person complimented?

What did you think and feel about the praise or compliment?

Did you listen carefully to the praise or compliment?

How did you express your thanks for the compliment?

Did you deserve the praise or compliment?

Thinking report: A situation or event where you had a chance to praise or compliment someone and you did not. Then do a rethinking report on the same event where you give a compliment.

THINKING REPORT	RETHINKING REPORT
Describe the event:	
Your thoughts:	
Your feelings:	
Your attitudes and beliefs:	
The outcome:	

SESSION 13

SOCIAL AND RELATIONSHIP

SKILLS BUILDING

LEARNING PROBLEM SOLVING

INTRODUCTION AND SESSION OBJECTIVES

PROBLEMS ARE PART OF LIFE. Each day we are faced with problems to solve. Problems involving other people and our relationships are often the most difficult to solve. Problems that touch us emotionally or that affect our core beliefs and attitudes are particularly difficult to solve.

Problems can happen that do not necessarily involve other people. Sometimes the solutions to the problem may not involve other people. You misplace your billfold and you go through solving the problem of finding it without anyone involved.

Most often, solutions do involve other people. One of the authors of this manual was returning from a trip to China. He discovered that he had left his appointment book in the hotel in Hong Kong. Panic set in because the book had all of his appointments for the coming week. His first impulse was to blame his wife for not checking the hotel room more closely. *Error in thinking: Blaming.* It wasn't her appointment book.

Several problems were faced. The appointments and times for next week had to be identified. An effort had to be made to locate the appointment book. Using the problem solving skills outlined in this session, a number of different problems were dealt with, thanks to the help of several people. The hotel staff found the appointment book, faxed the appointment pages for the coming two weeks, and arrangements were made to mail the book to the author. Problem solved!

Often, we problem solve *on the spur* of the moment (impulsively) without taking time. We often fail to see different solutions. We fail to get the facts. We tend to keep our attention on the person we are problem solving with rather than the problem. One way we have learned to solve problems is to *use alcohol or other drugs*. Good problem solving skills can keep us from getting frustrated, angry, depressed, away from relapse and even recidivism (driving while impaired). Solving problems is one of the keys to preventing relapse and recidivism.

OBJECTIVES OF THIS SESSION:
- Learn to apply the basic steps of problem solving.
- Learn to consider different solutions to problems.
- Learn how to cooperate and to look for solutions for the good of everyone.
- Look at the idea of finding new choices or alternatives to your thinking and behavior.

WE WILL START WITH THESE ACTIVITIES:

- Review Worksheets 32 and 33, page 121 and 122.
- Review the thinking report on missing a compliment, *Worksheet 34, page 122.*
- Do the *CB MAP Exercise.*

SESSION CONTENT AND FOCUS

A. WHAT IS A PROBLEM?

▶ A problem is an action, situation, or circumstance that causes you difficulty. The difficulty might be:

- not getting your way in a situation or not being sure what is expected of you;
- with another person over how things should be done or what actions to take;
- a difference between your goal and the goal of someone close - usually there is a goal attached to our problem;
- losing something important.

▶ When faced with problems, we may have physical symptoms such as our heart beats faster, we sweat, we cry, we get angry.

▶ Most problems involve other people. Some problems are serious, others are easy to solve. Sometimes we know we have a problem but we are unsure what it is. We get anxious and uneasy until we can clearly see the problem or the cause of the problem.

▶ *Example:* John's driver's license is suspended. He usually has a friend take him to work. This morning the friend is sick. So he's driving his friend's car to work. He hears a siren and sees in his rearview mirror a police car behind him, red lights flashing. John has a problem; does he pull over or run? He gets sweaty, his heart beats fast. What should John do?

John has a GOAL to get to where he is going but he also wants to stay out of jail. The police car presents an OBSTACLE to achieving his goal. Goals and obstacles are parts of problems. John thinks, decides that if he doesn't stop, his problems will be worse than not getting to his job on time. He pulls over. The policeman had just received an emergency call and whizzes by him. But is John's problem really over? What does he do now? Is the problem only not getting stopped on his way to work?

▶ A problem may only be in our thinking. This is the best place to solve our problem. We solve it in our heads before it takes place in our actions.

B. HERE ARE THE SIMPLE STEPS OF PROBLEM SOLVING

1. Identify and define the problem.

- ▶ Get all the facts.
- ▶ Study the problem.
- ▶ Have you been here before? Is the problem similar to one you had before?

2. What is your goal?

- What do you want?
- What is it you don't like?
- What do you want the short-term outcome to be?
- What do you want the long-term outcome to be?

3. Look at different solutions or alternatives.

- Brainstorm the solutions and come up with everything you can think of.
- What strengths do you have that will help you solve the problem?
- Get other people's ideas as to solutions.
- They don't have to be good solutions when brainstorming, just good ideas.
- What action should I take?
- What gets in the way of solving the problem - the obstacles?
- Do a solution ladder putting the best one at the top and the least desirable one at the bottom.
- Always match the solution with the outcome that you want.
- If others are involved, try to pick a solution that is win-win for everyone.

4. Choose the best solution and start the action — work the solution.

- As you work the solution, different approaches or new ideas may come up.
- Stop from time to time to see how the solution is working.
- Put the new ideas to work but keep with the solution you have chosen unless it's not working.
- If it is not working, start over, be flexible.

5. Study the outcome or results.

- Was it in your best interest?
- Did everyone gain from the outcome?
- Could you have done something differently? What will you do next time?
- Problem solving is a spiral. You never end up where you started. A new problem may come from solving the old one.

The problem solving cycle in the picture below shows that the outcome of problem solving never brings you back to where you started. You usually arrive at new levels of understanding and possibly new problems to be solved. As you study the outcome, always ask: Are you and others around you better off? Was it a win-win outcome?

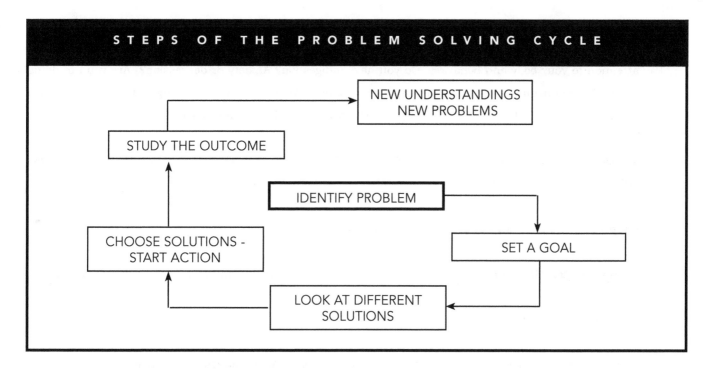

C. LEARNING TO APPLY DIFFERENT CHOICES

Think outside the box. Having different plans to choose from allows you to think in many different directions. You may have learned to do one kind of thing in a certain situation. Change that choice. It is in your power. Here is how to apply this *different choice method.*

1. **Learn to be aware you are making a decision - a choice: stop and think.** Don't rush into a solution. When you can make a decision, you have choices. Practice this. Even in the simple things. "I can decide to go to the grocery store first or the hardware store." You look at the alternatives.

2. **Get information.** Take your time. Details are important. Brainstorm all the possible answers. "What do I still need to know?" "What else might be contributing to the situation?" "What is another way I can think of this?" What are the possible outcomes?"

3. **Make your decision - your choice.**

4. **Look at the outcome** - Did it save time to go to the grocery store first? Replay the tape. What would be different had you gone to the hardware store first? Always think - *"I have many choices."* We often give up making changes because the problem seems too big or we see only one solution. We can solve any problem. Think outside the box.

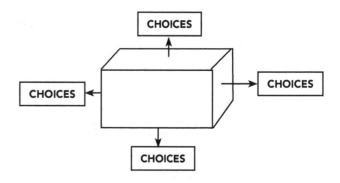

D. HOW DO WE KNOW WE HAVE A PROBLEM?

Pay attention to your body and behavior. Do you have indigestion? Anxiety or depression? Are you not doing work as well or not acting as you would like with your family? Are you not getting along with other people? Do they seem to avoid you? If you have these discomforts, you probably have a problem.

E. KEEP YOUR PROBLEM SOLVING SOLUTION FOCUSED. THESE ARE THE APPROACHES IN SOLUTION-FOCUSED PROBLEM SOLVING

1. **Keep your attention on the problem and not the person.**

2. **Keep your attention on the needs and interests of people involved and not on the positions they take.**

3. **Don't argue about the positions people take.**

4. **Pick solutions for the gain of all, and not just for yourself. Make solutions win-win.**

GOOD PROBLEM SOLVING GIVES YOU SELF-CONTROL. SELF-CONTROL LEADS TO POSITIVE OUTCOMES.

SESSION ACTIVITY AND HOMEWORK

A. **Exercise:** John would like to party with his friend Cliff who always drinks. When he goes out and drinks with Cliff, he usually puts himself at risk of getting into trouble. Apply the lessons above to this example.

B. Complete *Work Sheet 35,* page 129. Choose a problem you are now having and apply the steps of problem solving.

C. Thinking Report using *Work Sheet 36, page 130.* Think back on a problem you have had in the past. Do a thinking report. Do you want a different outcome? What thoughts do you need to have to produce a different outcome?

D. Update your Master Skills List and your skill mastery level.

E. Do your *AOD Weekly Monitoring Chart* for the coming week.

CLOSURE PROCESS GROUP

Share some of your past problems that were made worse because you did not apply the skills of problem solving.

Problem solving: Pick a problem that you are now having. Go through the steps below. See these simple steps for studying and coming up with solutions to this problem.

1. Identify or describe the problem:

2. What is your goal?

3. Look at different solutions - brainstorm:

4. What are the obstacles - what gets in the way of solving the problem?

5. Pick a solution:

6. Pick a solution and take action - put it to work:

7. Study the outcomes - how did it work?

Thinking report: Take one problem you have had in the past. What was the event, the thoughts, feeling and beliefs? What was the outcome? Do a rethinking report on this problem.

THINKING REPORT	RETHINKING REPORT
Describe the event:	
Your thoughts:	
Your feelings:	
Your attitudes and beliefs:	
The outcome:	

SESSION 14

SOCIAL AND RELATIONSHIP SKILLS BUILDING

ASSERTIVENESS SKILLS DEVELOPMENT

OVERVIEW AND SESSION OBJECTIVES

IN THE LAST FEW SESSIONS we have learned that we can have successful and positive relationships with others through using the skills of:

▶ effective communication;

▶ learning to start and continue difficult conversations;

▶ giving and receiving positive reinforcements; and

▶ effective problem solving.

These skills are helpful in building healthy and successful relationships because they *consider the needs and welfare of others as well as your own needs and welfare.* They are skills that help us CARE about ourselves and others. They are skills that help us to be responsible to ourselves, to others and to the community.

Getting our needs met as well as helping others get their needs met is one of the most important parts of living. This involves how we approach our relationships with others. Successful problem solving, getting our needs met and having successful relationships all depend on what kind of *action style* we take when relating to others. Persons with a history of alcohol or other drug use problems often need to improve their skills of how to get their needs met in healthy and meaningful ways. They have difficulty *setting limits* on their own behaviors and on the expectations of others - such as the expectation that they drink or use other drugs. How you approach your relationships with others will decide the success of the outcomes of your relationships.

We will look at three different styles of relating to others that most often do not lead to positive outcomes for yourself and for others. We will then learn a way or a style to approach our relationships with others that have greater chances of leading to positive outcomes. This approach may help you to maintain positive relationships and get positive outcomes in your relationships with others. This approach may also make a difference as to whether you relapse or recidivate (go back to driving while impaired).

OBJECTIVES OF THIS SESSION:

▶ Learn about three ways of relating to others that often lead to negative or conflictive outcomes in relationships.

▶ Learn and practice the relationship approach and skills of *being assertive.*

WE WILL START THIS SESSION BY:

▶ Doing the *CB MAP Exercise* with someone using an event that requires solving a problem.

▶ Review the work you did on your *AOD Weekly Monitoring Chart.*

SESSION CONTENT AND FOCUS

A. RELATING ASSERTIVENESS SKILL DEVELOPMENT TO YOUR MASTER PROFILE AND MASTER ASSESSMENT PLAN

If you rated yourself high on AOD use to cope with social discomfort and relationships, you have high needs for assertiveness training. Do you need to add this to your Master Assessment Plan?

B. THREE WAYS OF RELATING TO OTHERS THAT DO NOT LEAD TO PROBLEM SOLVING, RESOLVING CONFLICTS AND FULFILLING YOUR NEEDS AND THE NEEDS OF OTHERS

1. **FLIGHT:** *Avoid* the problem or be *passive* in problem solving and conflicts. Passive persons:

   ▶ store up their feelings;
   ▶ give up their rights when there is any conflict with what someone else wants;
   ▶ do not let others know what they are thinking or feeling;
   ▶ do not get what they want at their own expense;
   ▶ may get depressed or feel rejected;
   ▶ have to put out more and "pay" more in the long run; and
   ▶ may get people mad at them.

2. **FIGHT:** To attack others or get aggressive. Persons who are aggressive:

   ▶ Protect their own rights, but get what they want at the expense of others.
   ▶ Make others "pay."
   ▶ Cause others to get angry and to get even often in a passive-aggressive way.
   ▶ In the long run, the aggressive person ends up losing closeness and relationships and does not get meaningful relationship needs met.

3. **FAKE:** To be *passive-aggressive.*

   ▶ This falls between avoiding and being aggressive.
   ▶ Passive-aggressive persons are not direct in approaching problems. They express anger through "the silent treatment" or "slamming doors."
   ▶ They fail to express needs in a way that other people can respond to them.
   ▶ Passive-aggressive people don't get what they want at the expense of themselves and others.
   ▶ Both others and the person "pays."

These approaches to relationships most often **fail** to give positive outcomes or results. *None of these get your needs met in healthy ways.* All three methods drive people away. Persons who use these styles of relating will often drink or use other drugs in an effort to have their needs met. Yet, AOD use will only strengthen these styles of relating to others.

Is DWI behavior both *passive-aggressive* and *aggressive behavior.?* Discuss this in your group.

C. WHAT IS A HEALTHY RELATIONSHIP STYLE CHOICE?

1. **FAIR:** Learning to be *assertive*.

   - The *assertive* person looks after and protects his or her rights, but also respects other people's right to do the same.
   - By being *assertive,* you make an effort to get your needs met, but not at the expense of others.
   - Others do not "pay."
   - Works for a win-win solution.
   - The goal of being *assertive* is that both you and other people have their needs met. It is a way of CARING.
   - You drive with CARE when you use *assertive skills* in driving.

2. **The 10 keys to being assertive. Put a check in the box by those that are easy for you to do. If you have less than five checks, you probably are finding it difficult to be assertive. The more checked, the more assertive you can be.**

   - ❑ 1) Recognize your rights in a situation without trespassing on the rights of others.
   - ❑ 2) Know how to clearly state your opinions and what it is you want from others.
   - ❑ 3) Keep in mind the needs of others as you get your own needs met.
   - ❑ 4) Be flexible and give, yet at the same time, continue to make your position clear. Be willing to compromise.
   - ❑ 5) Avoid blaming; avoid using "you" messages.
   - ❑ 6) State how you feel and think; use "I" messages.
   - ❑ 7) Have your goals clearly in mind. Know what you want.
   - ❑ 8) Become part of the solution and not part of the problem.
   - ❑ 9) Once you make a decision, stick with what you have decided. Don't relive or continually rehash "what might have been."
   - ❑ 10) Confront the issues head-on. Attack the problem and not the person.

D. PRACTICING WHAT YOU HAVE LEARNED

Exercise: You want to take a Friday afternoon to attend your son's football game. You are out of vacation time. You have two days of sick time. The football game is two weeks away. Work is busy and the boss is not giving time away easily. Group members will role play each of these four ways to handle the problem.

- ▶ *Avoiding* - FLIGHT.
- ▶ *Aggressive* - FIGHT.
- ▶ *Passive-aggressive* - FAKE.
- ▶ *Assertiveness* - FAIR. **Apply the 10 keys to being assertive in this situation.**

Exercises: Role play the following examples using all four methods to solve the problem. When using the *assertive approach,* keep in mind the 10 ways of being assertive. After each method, decide whether the goals of the person were met.

- ▶ *Example:* Your boss promised you a bonus for working on the weekend. The extra money does not appear on your paycheck. The goal is to get the bonus without offending the boss.
- ▶ You have paid all your bills, but a department store says your bill is delinquent.
- ▶ You buy an appliance for full price and a day later see it advertised for one third off.
- ▶ You rode to the bar with a friend. When you are leaving, your friend wants you to drive because he has had too much to drink. But so have you. Your goal is that neither of you drive.

Exercise: Your group leader will have one or more group members choose a real situation to role play. Keep the focus on the assertive style. Have the group give feedback and suggestions regarding how the *assertive character* could have achieved the desired outcome.

SESSION AND HOMEWORK ACTIVITIES

A. In group, do a *Thinking Report* using *Work Sheet 37,* page 136. Choose a situation in which you could have been assertive but you were not. Describe the event or situation, your thoughts, feelings, beliefs and the outcome.

B. Using *Work Sheet 38,* page 136, do a Re-thinking Report on the situation in *Work Sheet 37.*

C. Update your Master Skills List, page 31. Update your skills ratings.

D. Do your *AOD Weekly Monitoring Chart.*

CLOSURE PROCESS GROUP

Thinking report: Choose a situation in which you could have been assertive but you were not.

Describe the event:

Your thoughts:

Your feelings:

Your attitudes and beliefs:

The outcome:

Re-Thinking report: Re-think how you might approach the situation you used in *Work Sheet 35*. Change your thinking. What feelings do you now have? What beliefs do you now need to think in this way? What do you think the outcome will now be?.

Describe the event:

Your thoughts:

Your feelings:

Your attitudes and beliefs:

The outcome:

SESSION 15

SOCIAL AND RELATIONSHIP SKILLS BUILDING

LEARNING AND PRACTICING REFUSAL SKILLS

OVERVIEW AND SESSION OBJECTIVES

AS YOU MAKE efforts to change, each day you will be confronted with high-risk exposures that can lead to relapse and recidivism. Most dangerous are high-risk situations in which you are confronted with drinking or using other drugs. One is the pressure from peers to drink, particularly in social settings or bars away from home. Learning to "just say no" to the offer of drugs and/or alcohol is frequently not enough, especially if you are still not sure if you want to change your use patterns. Being aware of your old patterns that put you at risk is important. *Difficult situations will still come up,* even if you have been successful in avoiding old companions and the peer pressures. People who are unaware of what you have been through may tempt you into going back to old patterns. Some who are aware could be thoughtless and even try to force that on you. Different situations will present different difficulties. Practice in how to refuse to take part in situations that can lead to relapse and recidivism will be our topic in this session.

OBJECTIVES OF THIS SESSION

▶ Review some of the important parts of our work on relapse and recidivism that we did in **DWC Education** and in previous sessions of this program.

▶ Learn and practice refusal skills to cope with these high-risk situations.

▶ Learn and practice refusal skills to cope with high-risk situations and high-risk thinking.

▶ Try to spot the situations that are high risk for AOD use or relapse into impaired driving that make it difficult to refuse drinking or use of other drugs.

WE WILL START THIS SESSION BY:

▶ Doing the CB MAP Exercise. One group member will be asked to use one event where he/she was aggressive.

▶ Reviewing the Thinking and Re-thinking Report done in the last session on *Worksheets 37* and *38* involving a situation where you could have been assertive, but were not.

SESSION CONTENT AND FOCUS

A. RELATING REFUSAL SKILL DEVELOPMENT TO YOUR MASTER PROFILE AND MAP

If you rated yourself high on *convivial* or *gregarious* drinking or drinking to cope with social discomfort, it may be difficult for you to put into practice drink-refusal skills. Do you need to add new problems to your MAP?

B. REVIEW OF IMPORTANT IDEAS ABOUT RELAPSE AND RECIDIVISM

1. Relapse is a return to a pattern of AOD use that causes problems or harm to yourself or others.

2. Recidivism is returning to any involvement in impaired driving.

3. High-risk exposures are high-risk situations, thoughts, emotions, attitudes and beliefs that lead to relapse and recidivism.

4. One high-risk situation is pressure from peers to become involved in AOD use that can lead to relapse or to impaired driving.

C. PEER PRESSURE

One of our most important needs is to be accepted by our peers. This need leaves us open to PEER PRESSURE.

1. **Peer pressure has its roots in the animal world when it was safer to be in a herd or a flock to be protected from other animals.** Being part of the group is necessary for survival. This need for acceptance and to belong carried over into the human world.

2. **The conflict comes when standing up for what is best and safe for you goes against the needs and pressure from your group or peers.** Can you stand up for your rights and do what is best for you and still be accepted by your peers?

   ▶ Peers and groups are very powerful in "talking" you into doing what you don't want to or shouldn't do.

   ▶ The bottom line is that you are responsible for your choices and behaviors, not your peers or group.
   ▶ Self-control is doing what is best for you, not doing what your peers or group want you to do.

3. **Peer pressure is a trigger for relapse and recidivism.**

   ▶ It is difficult to say "no" to friends who want you to get high with them, or have "a few." You have a strong need to be accepted, to be "safe." But does being part of the group always make you safe?
   ▶ Your risk of driving while impaired is much higher if you are with friends who are drinking. You are very likely to do what the group wants you to do. You care for your peers. But does driving impaired under peer pressure make you safe and CARING?

D. A POSITIVE WAY TO HANDLE PEER PRESSURE IS BEING ASSERTIVE

   ▶ Assertiveness is the sure way of making your own decisions, of getting a positive outcome, and not being "talked into" actions that are not for your best interest.
   ▶ When assertive, you handle group and peer pressure while at the same time keep the good will of your friends.
   ▶ An important piece of being assertive and managing peer pressure is using refusal skills.

E. TIPS FOR LEARNING AND PRACTICING REFUSAL SKILLS

Your approach to refusal behavior will depend on your relapse prevention goal of not returning to a pattern of use that leads to AOD problem outcomes; or not using at all - *total abstinence.* It also depends on your recidivism prevention goal: prevent legal recidivism or zero tolerance-zero risk. If you have chosen a *relapse prevention goal* of avoiding drinking patterns that can lead to problem outcomes, then it will be important that you make the refusal ideas fit that goal. Here are some tips in using refusal skills.

1. **First, what are your thoughts?** Remember, your thoughts lead to saying "yes" or to making a refusal statement or saying "no." Are you thinking, "Maybe I'll stay and have a few more?" Or, "I'm going home now?"

2. **Say "no" without hesitation and in a firm, clear voice.** Think "no" first. Your thoughts might convince yourself that it might be all right or fun "just this once." Saying "no" after having a few is more difficult.

3. **Look at the person directly.** This makes it clear that you do not want to relapse; or, you are not going to have more than two because you will be at risk for impaired driving.

4. **Don't feel guilty about refusing**. You won't hurt anyone by saying "no," but you could hurt yourself by saying "yes." Remember the problems your DWI arrest caused you.

5. **Ask the person putting pressure on you to change their behavior of asking or putting pressure on you**. A friend will hear your message.

6. **Make it clear to the person what you have to lose by saying yes.** Let people know "This is what I have to lose."

7. **Make your "no" statement and change the subject.** Don't debate with the other person. That means you are wavering; you are debating with yourself.

8. **Don't make excuses.** An excuse means you won't now, but you might later. Under some situations, it may be acceptable to make an excuse. Think of some circumstances where this would be true.

9. **Choose an action and follow through.** Do something else. Go to a movie, go for a walk, to dinner, or have coffee and talk. "I don't have to go the bar to have fun."

Exercise: Using different situations where you are offered opportunity to drink or use drugs, practice these refusal skills. Give feedback to the person role playing as to his or her effectiveness.

Exercise: Role play different situations where you are at risk of drinking and driving. Practice refusal skills. When it comes to drinking and driving, the most important person you refuse is yourself.

F. **STEPS FOR REFUSAL**

1. **THINK** about the positive outcomes for making a refusal response and the bad outcomes if you don't refuse.

    ◗   Think, "I'm going to refuse, I'm not going to do that."
    ◗   You may have to do some "tough" self-talk if you are wavering some.
    ◗   Make up your mind and be firm with your thinking. You're the one you have to refuse. Making up your mind to refuse is 80 percent of the battle.

2. **DECIDE** on your refusal response.

    ◗   Look at the different ways you can think about saying "no" to behaviors that can lead to bad outcomes for you.
    ◗   Then, choose one response that is logical and makes sense to you.
    ◗   Use strong "I" messages. Take responsibility for your refusal response. Avoid "you" responses.

3. **STATE** your response clearly and directly.

    ◗   Make it clear what your actions will be.
    ◗   Make it more than just a "no." "I'm not going to bars any more." "I'm not driving after I've had even one drink."
    ◗   Make it clear you are not refusing the other person but only refusing a certain action or activity.
    ◗   Make it clear you are refusing to let yourself do something that can lead to a bad outcome for you.

4. **ACT** on your choice.

    ◗   The action is more than just your statement. It is doing something.
    ◗   Let your action offer alternatives. "I won't stop for a drink, but let's get some coffee."

5. **FOLLOW THROUGH** with your action.

    ◗   **Bring your action to a positive conclusion.**
    ◗   **"Look down the road." The follow-through will carry over to the next time you have to choose to refuse an action that will lead to a bad outcome.**

G. **IDENTIFYING HIGH-RISK SITUATIONS FOR AOD USE AND SITUATIONS IN WHICH REFUSAL WILL BE DIF-FICULT.** Learning the skills of refusal will also mean that you know the situations in which you put to work the REFUSAL SKILLS.

Exercise: Do *Work Sheet 39,* page 143. Identify situations that you think will place you at high risk for AOD use or a getting into a pattern of AOD problem outcomes or that are setups for DWI conduct. These will be **situations in which it will be difficult to refuse or to say "NO."**

H. PRACTICE CHANGING YOUR THINKING THAT LEADS TO A REFUSAL STATEMENT

Exercise: Use *Work Sheet 40,* page 144, and recall several situations where you were offered alcohol or other drugs and you said "yes" and drank or used. Describe the situation. What were your **acceptance thoughts?** What did you say to accept? Change the thought to a refusal thought that will lead to a refusal statement.

Remember: self-control leads to positive outcomes. We get self-control by controlling and changing our thoughts.

SESSION OR HOMEWORK ACTIVITIES

A. Update your Master Skills List and skill levels, page 31. Are you improving on the skills you have learned?

B. Do your AOD Weekly Monitoring Chart.

C. Practice assertiveness and refusal skills this week.

CLOSURE PROCESS GROUP

Discuss with other group members the difference between the high-risk exposures that lead to drinking and high risk exposures that lead to drinking and driving.

INVITE YOUR SIGNIFICANT OTHER/INTIMATE PARTNER TO THE NEXT SESSION.

List of high-risk - difficult-to-refuse situations. Identify situations that you think will place you at high risk for AOD use or a getting into a pattern of AOD problem outcomes or that are setups for DWI conduct. These will be **situations in which it will be difficult to refuse or to say "NO."**

HIGH-RISK/DIFFICULT TO REFUSE SITUATIONS FOR DRINKING OR USING DRUGS OR FOR RELAPSE INTO PATTERNS OF AOD PROBLEM OUTCOMES	ARE THESE SETUPS FOR DWI BEHAVIOR?

WORKSHEET 40

DESCRIBE SITUATION	YOUR "YES" THOUGHTS	YOUR "YES" STATEMENTS	YOUR "NO" OR REFUSAL THOUGHT
ONE:			
TWO:			
THREE:			

144

S E S S I O N   1 6

SOCIAL SKILLS BUILDING

DEVELOPING AND KEEPING INTIMATE AND CLOSE RELATIONSHIPS

INTRODUCTION AND SESSION OBJECTIVES

AN IMPORTANT TRIGGER for relapse and recidivism is *conflict in our close and intimate relationships.* Relationship problems, loneliness and lack of relationships can contribute to DWI behavior. People who have problems in relationships or who do not have close supportive relationships will often seek "a second family" with drinking friends at parties or the bar. This is high risk for relapse and recidivism.

In many of our sessions, we have worked on developing good communication skills. These skills can help strengthen our intimate and closest relationships. Sometimes it is more difficult to solve problems with those with whom we are close than with strangers. This is often true because of the emotional ties we have with those with whom we are close. We often try to avoid anger; or we become angry because our partner or the relationship does not meet our needs and expectations. We may fear failing in our relationships.

Our fixed expectations of the other person may also keep us from having good communication with that person. We may have *leaned on alcohol or other drugs* to deal with the problems and feelings that come from relationships with people we love and with whom we are close.

Part of developing good communication between people in intimate relationships is to deal *openly with sexual problems or issues.* This is a sensitive area, and you may want to deal with some of these things in a separate session with your counselor and your intimate partner.

REMEMBER, THERE IS POWER IN COMMUNICATION. IT IS THE POWER OF TALKING AND THE POWER OF LISTENING.

The purpose of this session is to help you understand how important good communication is in developing and maintaining intimate and close relationships. We will review some of these basic communication skills. We will also look at what we learned about having a good balance between *closeness* and *separateness* in close relationships. We recommend that you bring your "significant other," spouse, roommate or intimate partner to this session.

OBJECTIVES FOR THIS SESSION
▶ Help you see how important good communication is in intimate and close relationships.
▶ Look at ways to improve closeness in our intimate partner relationship.
▶ Look at the importance of maintaining the balance between closeness and intimacy.

WE WILL START THIS SESSION WITH THE FOLLOWING ACTIVITIES.

▶ Introduce the "significant other" guests.

▶ One or two group members will be asked to do the CB MAP exercise, using peer pressure as the event.

▶ Take a few minutes to review and change, if necessary, your Master Profile (MP) and to review and update your Master Assessment Plan (MAP).

▶ Have group members share one or two of the most important ideas or skills that they have learned in the DWC program.

SESSION CONTENT AND FOCUS

A. SOME IMPORTANT IDEAS ABOUT DEVELOPING AND KEEPING INTIMATE AND CLOSE RELATIONSHIPS

1. Developing and keeping healthy intimacy requires that we keep a healthy balance between these two powerful needs:

▶ a need to belong, to be close, to share with others and to have intimacy; and

▶ a need to be separate, to be ourselves, to be different.

2. Two communication skills that we learned in Session 10.

▶ **Active Sharing.** This is *self-directed communication* and is based on using the skills of:
  • *sharing about yourself* - using "I" messages; and
  • *receiving feedback* from others about you.

▶ **Active Listening.** This is *other-directed communication* and is based on using the skills of:
  • *inviting* the other person to share by using open statements or open questions; and
  • *reflecting* back what you hear the other person saying so they know that you have heard them and are interested in what they have said to you.

3. Two important parts of active sharing and active listening that we learned in Sessions 11 and 12 are very important in developing and keeping close and intimate relationships.

▶ *Starting conversations,* talking and sharing stories and experiences.

▶ *Giving positive reinforcement* such as compliments.

Exercise: Practice the skills of active listening and active sharing in the group. One group member will do active sharing and the other will respond back with active listening skills.

B. PATHWAYS AND SKILLS TO DEVELOPING AND KEEPING HEALTHY INTIMACY

These 10 pathways and skills will help you build love, commitment and respect in your relationships.

1. **Be proactive and active in the relationship.**

   ◗ Put energy into the relationship.
   ◗ Make things happen. Do your share of planning activities and see that they happen.

2. **Let your partner be proactive and active.**

   ◗ Respect your partner's making things happen.
   ◗ Support your partner's effort to *energize* the relationship.

3. **Interact rather than react to what your partner does.**

   ◗ Use the skills of *active listening* and *active sharing* to interact.
   ◗ When you only react, you make your intimate partner responsible rather than taking responsibility for your thoughts, feelings and actions.

4. **Keep a balance between closeness and separateness and avoid co-dependency.**

   ◗ Be OK even when your partner is not OK.
   ◗ When you are not OK, let your partner be OK.
   ◗ Each must safeguard the self but also the relationship.

5. **Remember win-win when working on differences or resolving conflicts.**

   ◗ Keep the focus on the problem, not on the other person.
   ◗ State the other person's position or side.
   ◗ Talk about yourself, not the other person.
   ◗ Use "I" messages, not "you" messages.
   ◗ After a conflict is resolved, be sure that each of you is better off.

6. **Help the other person be successful and celebrate that success.**

7. Combine your strengths for the good of each other and the relationship.

▶ Each of you have different strengths. Profit from each other's strengths.

▶ Be proud of the other person's strengths and achievements.

▶ What most likely attracted you to each other was the strength of your differences.

▶ Remember, opposites attract. *Profit from those opposites.*

8. Don't let things build up.

▶ It is easy to let things build up between you.

▶ To keep from being bothered about what happens between the two of you and to keep them from building up, *tell your partner* what bothers you.

▶ Don't expect your partner to read your mind. Communicate what you want, feel or think.

9. Keep your relationship fresh and romantic.

▶ Always do something new, something different.

▶ Take trips, go to different places, have fun.

▶ Keep up the romance. Remember, romance brought you together.

▶ See physical and sexual intimacy as sharing each other's physical being and as more than having sex.

▶ Take part in healthy play - to move freely in space together.

10. Give and receive positive reinforcement.

▶ Give compliments and praise.

▶ Be open to receiving compliments and praise.

▶ Express things you appreciate about the other person.

▶ Make the positive outweigh the negative. Otherwise, it will be a negative relationship.

▶ The relationship is made better if positive expressions are there. It is particularly true for sexual and physical intimacy. Sexual intimacy can't take place without *positive feelings* between the couple.

C. KEEPING THE BALANCE

A healthy and balanced relationship allows each person to have their separateness while at the same time keeping closeness. A relationship often gets so close, we feel swallowed up. When we feel we are losing our separateness and our uniqueness, we will fight closeness. Yet, you need to give part of yourself to the relationship. You can't have it all your way. Three different relationships are shown in the picture below.

Exercise: Do *Work Sheet 41,* page 151. If your significant other or intimate partner is in the session, do it separately and then compare your findings. Answer the questions in the *Work Sheet.* If you are not in an intimate relationship, then pick someone you are close with in your life.

Exercise: Do *Work Sheet 42,* page 152. *Looking at your Closeness and Separateness.* If present, have your significant partner do the *Work Sheet.* If you do not have a significant other, do the *Work Sheet* based on what you would like in a relationship. Share your findings with each other and with the group.

RELATIONSHIP AND BALANCE

CIRCLE ONE: ENMESHED
Relationship dominates
individuals, little separation or
individuality

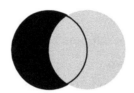

CIRCLE THREE: BALANCED
Healthy balance between closeness and
separateness, between
individuality and relationship

CIRCLE TWO: DETACHED
Individual needs to dominate,
little giving to the relationship

D. PRACTICE ACTIVE SHARING AND ACTIVE LISTENING

Exercise: If your significant other is present in the session, practice the skills of *active sharing* and *active listening.* Have one do the active sharing and the other do the active listening. Change roles. If you do not have a significant other present, have someone play the role of that significant other.

Exercise: Give one group member feedback as to how that member has made self-improvement or change. Then, with your significant other, just take time to talk and share whatever comes to your mind. If you do not have a significant other at the session, have group members play the part of the significant other. Reverse roles.

SESSION HOMEWORK ACTIVITIES

A. Do your Master Skills List and skills mastery levels, page 31. Update your ratings.

B. Do your *AOD Weekly Monitoring Chart.*

C. Look at your *Master Profile.* If you rated yourself high on *social irresponsibility* as a negative consequence of AOD use, and high on *Social-Relationship Problems,* you probably have had problems in intimate partnership relationships. Do you need to add to your MAP based on what you learned in this session?

CLOSURE PROCESS GROUP

Share your thoughts and feelings about what you did in this session.

Looking at the relationship with your significant other or intimate partner. Draw the relationship you and your intimate partner have. If you are not in an intimate relationship, pick someone you are close to in your life.

A. DRAW CIRCLES HERE:

B. REFLECT ON:

1. What do you think about what you see?

2. Why are things like they are?

3. How would you like the relationship? Draw another set of circles below if you want a different balance between closeness and separateness.

Looking at your closeness and separateness. In one column, write those things that represent intimacy and closeness (for example, going to movies together). Then list those things that you do separate from the relationship that keep your own sense of self and identity.

THINGS YOU DO THAT BRING YOU CLOSE OR TOGETHER.	WHAT DO YOU DO THAT IS SEPARATE FROM YOUR PARTNER?

SESSION 17

STRENGTHENING RECIDIVISM AND RELAPSE PREVENTION SKILLS

OVERVIEW AND SESSION OBJECTIVES

EACH DAY THAT YOU MEET your goal of preventing DWI behavior and relapse you become stronger. You achieved these goals because you have a **commitment** to making changes in your life. As you succeed in mastering the skills of cognitive self-control and change, you begin to take **ownership** of those changes. They become yours.

Because relapse and recidivism (R&R) are such important therapy topics, we are going to spend the next two sessions on R&R. Some of this session may be a review of what you learned and practiced in **DWC Education.** The main purpose of this session is to strengthen our relapse and recidivism prevention skills.

OBJECTIVES FOR THIS SESSION

▶ Review some important ideas about R&R and R&R prevention.

▶ Review the cognitive-behavioral map for relapse and recidivism.

▶ Look at your triggers for R&R.

▶ Understand the R&R prevention process and steps.

▶ Look at your high-risk thinking and situations and the skills you have used to deal with those situations.

WE WILL START THIS SESSION WITH:

▶ A review of your AOD Weekly Monitoring Chart;

▶ Doing the CB MAP Exercise.

▶ Update your Master Assessment Plan (MAP)

SESSION CONTENT

A. RELATING R&R PREVENTION TO YOUR MP AND MASTER ASSESSMENT PLAN - MAP.

Look at the *Alcohol and Other Drug Use Assessment* part of your *Master Profile (MP), Work Sheet 4,* page 32. The higher your scores on the *quantity-frequency* and *negative consequence* scales, the greater your risk for recidivism and relapse.

B. REVIEWING WHAT WE HAVE LEARNED ABOUT RECIDIVISM AND RELAPSE AND R&R PREVENTION

1. The process of DWI recidivism.

▶ **Legal recidivism** - driving with a BAC beyond legal limits or while under the influence of or impaired by other mind behavior-altering drugs. Society's prevention goal for you is to prevent legal recidivism.

- ▶ **"Zero tolerance-zero risk" recidivism,**- driving while having in your body any alcohol or other drugs not prescribed by a doctor.

- ▶ DWI recidivism is a gradual erosion process that begins when you become involved in high risk exposures that can lead to a pattern of impaired driving behavior. They are:

  - • **high-risk thinking** - thought habits and automatic thoughts that lead to thinking you can drink and drive such as "I'm OK to drive, I only had a couple;"
  - • **high-risk situations** - that lead to being involved in driving while impaired such as driving to a drinking party alone with no alternative but to drive yourself home;
  - • **high-risk feelings** - that have led to past impaired driving such as anger, "You won't stop me from driving," or depression, "I don't care"; and
  - • **high-risk attitudes and beliefs** - such as the attitude, "Screw 'em, no one tells me I can't drive," or the belief, "I'm never too drunk to drive."

- ▶ The erosion continues when high-risk thinking and high-risk behaviors (situations) become habit patterns. **UNLESS YOU CHANGE THESE HABIT PATTERNS, YOU ARE AT RISK FOR GETTING ANOTHER DWI CHARGE.**

- ▶ Again, write in the space below your recidivism prevention goal.

Exercise: Do *Work Sheet 43,* page 161 and list your high-risk thinking and high-risk situations that could have led to recidivism.

2. The Process of AOD Relapse.

- ▶ Relapse depends on your personal goal.

  - • If your goal is to *never take another drink or never use any other non-prescribed mind-altering drugs,* and you do use, you are **into relapse;** and you **have relapsed** when your use causes you problems or harm to yourself or others.
  - • If your goal is to *never allow alcohol or other drugs to cause you further problems in your life* and you go back to **a pattern of use that will lead** to problems or harm to yourself or others, you are into relapse; and if your use causes problems or harm to yourself or others, you have relapsed.

- ▶ You can relapse without driving. YET, RELAPSE IS ALWAYS HIGH RISK FOR DWI RECIDIVISM. IT IS THE FIRST STEP TO RECIDIVISM.

▶ AOD relapse is a gradual process of erosion that begins when you become involved in high-risk exposures that lead to a pattern of drinking or other drug use that is harmful to you or leads to DWI behavior. These high-risk exposures for relapse are:

- **high-risk thinking** or thought habits that in the past have led to AOD problems, such as "I'm going to a party and get drunk;"

- **high-risk situations** that led to AOD problems and abuse in the past and which make you think or feel that you need to use alcohol or other drugs, such as getting into conflict with your partner, going to a party where everyone gets high;

- **high-risk feelings** that led to AOD problems in the past such as feeling sad, feeling lonely, being angry at your spouse;

- **high-risk attitudes** and beliefs that led to AOD problems in the past such as the attitude, " I can handle my drinks," or the belief, " The only way I can feel good is to drink."

▶ The *erosion continues* when high-risk thinking and high-risk behavior (situations) become habit patterns.

▶ Write in the space below your relapse prevention goal.

Exercise: Do *Work Sheet 44,* page 161, and list your high-risk thinking and high-risk situations that could have led to relapse.

C. PREVENTING DWI RECIDIVISM AND RELAPSE

1. Triggers for recidivism and relapse.

Research has shown that 75 percent of the relapses by problem drinkers were related to three triggers or high-risk exposures.

▶ *High-risk negative or unpleasant thoughts and emotions* such as stress, depression, anger and stress

▶ *Interpersonal conflict* with someone close - high-risk situations.

▶ *Social or peer pressure* to drink or use drugs - high-risk situations.

Exercise: Review *Figure 1,* page 14, of *Session 1,* the cognitive-behavioral CB map for change. Do *Work Sheet 45,* page 162. This work sheet follows the CB map. For each of the three triggers described above, write down a situation that applies to you. Write your thoughts and feelings. What did you do or what was your action? Was it positive (helped you cope) or negative (led to relapse/recidivism)?

2. **The pathway to recidivism and relapse (R&R).**

Figure 9, **page 159, provides a picture of the pathways to relapse and recidivism (R&R).** They have their own separate pathways, but they are also linked together. Study the picture and then discuss how it might fit you.

Exercise: Look at the high-exposures in *Figure 9.* Have you experienced some not listed in the rectangles? Example: Is there a high-risk situation for recidivism you have experienced but is not given? If so, write it in. Share what you found with the group.

3. **The process and skills of relapse and recidivism (R&R) prevention.**

The R&R map. *Figure 10,* **page 160, gives you the map for relapse and recidivism prevention (RRP).** The left side of the map is similar to *Figure 9.* The right side is the *prevention path.* At each point you have choices. When confronted with high-risk situations, you can jump to the prevention side at any point. The keys to preventing relapse and recidivism are:

▶ manage high-risk thinking, attitudes and beliefs, by using all of the cognitive change and self-control skills you have learned;

▶ manage high-risk situations by using the relationship skills, community responsibility skills and community support resources learned in this program;

▶ manage high-risk feelings using skills learned in this program, to handle stress, anxiety and depression.

In **DWC Education,** you figured the cost of money and time of your DWI arrest.

▶ Your cost: $_____ You may have to go back to your DWI Education workbook for that cost.

▶ Your time: _____ hours

Ask yourself: DO I WANT TO GO THROUGH THAT AGAIN?

Explaining some important ideas in the R&R prevention map, *Figure 10.*

▶ **Expect positive outcomes:** You may expect going to the bar and having a few drinks will relax you, make you feel good. When the prospect of AOD use is hooked in with a positive outcome of AOD use, your chances of relapse or residivism skyrockets.

▶ **Self-Efficacy or Self-Mastery.** Your judgement about how well you cope with stressful or difficult situations. This is based on whether you have succeeded or failed in similar situations and how others judge or influence you. When you succeed, you increase your self-esteem.

- **Rule violation effect.** This is your reaction to *going against your rule* that you will not drink or you will not get back into a problem using pattern or you will never again drink and drive. You have been seeing yourself as following these rules, as "on the straight and narrow." Then you go against the rule. You drink. You drive and drink. You get another problem from drinking. That view of yourself now changes. You are now seeing your old self. So what are you? "Clean and sober" or "a problem drinker." You are in serious conflict. To solve this conflict, you may return to your old view of yourself - a problem drinker. The strength of this *rule violation* will depend on how strong you see yourself, your *self-mastery* or *efficacy,* how much guilt you feel and how much you blame your personal weaknesses for the cause of the R&R behavior. You may decide, "screw it, I took one drink, just as well get drunk."

- The keys to relapse and recidivism prevention are **strong coping and cognitive-behavioral skills** to manage high-risk exposures, which **gives you self-control**. SELF-CONTROL LEADS TO POSITIVE OUTCOMES.

Exercise: Use *Work Sheets 46 and 47,* page 163. Make a list of the thinking and action skills to prevent recidivism and relapse that you have been using and which have been working for you in the past three to six months. These skills are part of your R&R plan.

D. UPDATING YOUR MAP AND MASTER SKILL LIST

- Based on what you learned in this session, update your MAP.
- Update your skills list on page 31 and update your level of mastery on skills you learned.

HOMEWORK

A. Do your *AOD Weekly Monitoring Chart.*

B. Using *Worksheet 48,* page 164, do a thinking report on high-risk situations that can lead to R&R.

CLOSURE PROCESS GROUP

Share how you see your relapse and recidivism prevention goals now compared to when you were in DWC Education.

FIGURE 9

Pathways to relapse and recidivism.

PATHWAY TO RELAPSE HIGH-RISK EXPOSURES	PATHWAY TO RECIDIVISM HIGH-RISK EXPOSURES
HIGH-RISK SITUATIONS Relationship conflicts. Problems at work. Socialize with drinking friends. Attend drinking parties. Friends pressure you to drink.	**HIGH-RISK SITUATIONS** Attend drinking parties often. Drinking at the bar after driving to the bar alone. Run out of booze at home after having a few drinks. Drink at bar with friends.
HIGH-RISK THINKING No one really cares. Being unfairly treated. A few drinks will help. Not fair, can't drink. I don't fit in when I don't drink. A couple would feel good.	**HIGH-RISK THINKING** I only had two beers when I got my DWI. I've had a couple of beers but I can drive OK. Nobody is going to drive me home. I'm not too drunk to drive.
HIGH-RISK FEELINGS Happy over getting a raise. Feeling down and depressed. Angry at spouse and boss. I'm feeling stressed. Angry at everybody. Feeling lonely.	**HIGH-RISK FEELINGS** I don't care if I get caught. I don't feel quite so down drinking here with friends. I feel more accepted and relaxed here at the bar.
ATTITUDES AND BELIEFS To hell with everyone. Nothing works out. The world is not fair. I feel better when I drink. Drinking won't hurt me.	**ATTITUDES AND BELIEFS** Screw'em, I can drive OK. Nobody's going to tell me I can't drive. I'm not going to get caught.
RELAPSE PATTERN Frequent drinking at bar. Daily pattern of use. Into frequent/heavy use. Into a pattern that led to past problems.	**RECIDIVISM BEHAVIOR** Driving home after many drinks. Into pattern of driving with BAC above legal limit.
FULL RELAPSE HARMFUL AND DISRUPTIVE RESULTS FROM DRINKING.	**NEW DWI CITATION** CONVICTED OF ANOTHER DWI

Adapted with permission from G.H. Marlatt, 1985, Relapse Prevention: Theoretical rationale and overview. In G.A. Marlatt, & J.R. Gordon (Eds.), Relapse Prevention: Maintenance Strategies in the treatment of addictive behaviors (p. 38), Guilford Press.

FIGURE   10

Cognitive-behavioral map for relapse and recidivism
PREVENTION.

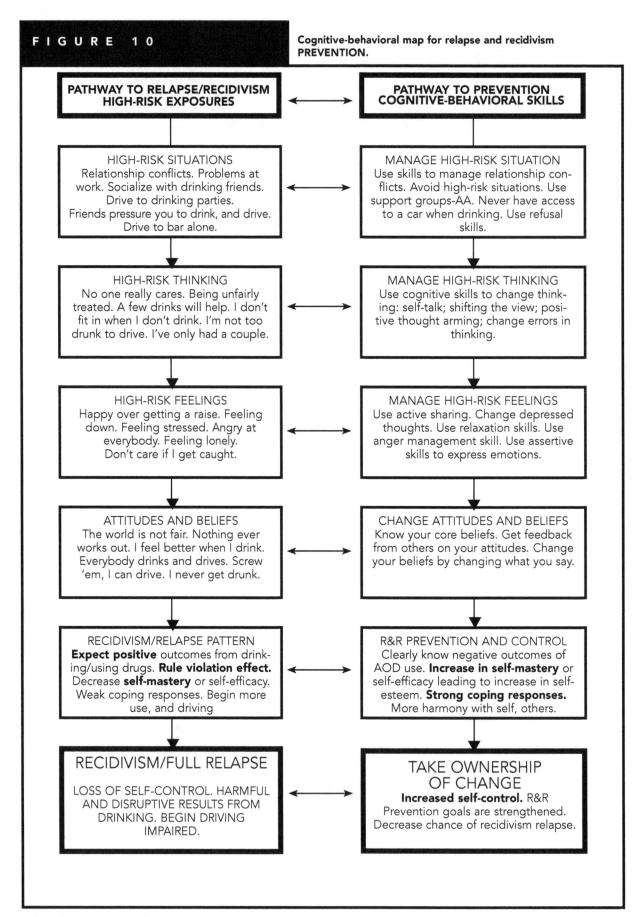

PATHWAY TO RELAPSE/RECIDIVISM
HIGH-RISK EXPOSURES ⟷ PATHWAY TO PREVENTION
COGNITIVE-BEHAVIORAL SKILLS

HIGH-RISK SITUATIONS
Relationship conflicts. Problems at
work. Socialize with drinking friends.
Drive to drinking parties.
Friends pressure you to drink, and drive.
Drive to bar alone. ⟷ MANAGE HIGH-RISK SITUATION
Use skills to manage relationship conflicts. Avoid high-risk situations. Use
support groups-AA. Never have access
to a car when drinking. Use refusal
skills.

HIGH-RISK THINKING
No one really cares. Being unfairly
treated. A few drinks will help. I don't
fit in when I don't drink. I'm not too
drunk to drive. I've only had a couple. ⟷ MANAGE HIGH-RISK THINKING
Use cognitive skills to change think-
ing: self-talk; shifting the view; positive thought arming; change errors in
thinking.

HIGH-RISK FEELINGS
Happy over getting a raise. Feeling
down. Feeling stressed. Angry at
everybody. Feeling lonely.
Don't care if I get caught. ⟷ MANAGE HIGH-RISK FEELINGS
Use active sharing. Change depressed
thoughts. Use relaxation skills. Use
anger management skill. Use assertive
skills to express emotions.

ATTITUDES AND BELIEFS
The world is not fair. Nothing ever
works out. I feel better when I drink.
Everybody drinks and drives. Screw
'em, I can drive. I never get drunk. ⟷ CHANGE ATTITUDES AND BELIEFS
Know your core beliefs. Get feedback
from others on your attitudes. Change
your beliefs by changing what you say.

RECIDIVISM/RELAPSE PATTERN
Expect positive outcomes from drink-
ing/using drugs. **Rule violation effect.**
Decrease **self-mastery** or self-efficacy.
Weak coping responses. Begin more
use, and driving ⟷ R&R PREVENTION AND CONTROL
Clearly know negative outcomes of
AOD use. **Increase in self-mastery** or
self-efficacy leading to increase in self-
esteem. **Strong coping responses.**
More harmony with self, others.

RECIDIVISM/FULL RELAPSE

LOSS OF SELF-CONTROL. HARMFUL
AND DISRUPTIVE RESULTS FROM
DRINKING. BEGIN DRIVING
IMPAIRED. ⟷ TAKE OWNERSHIP
OF CHANGE
Increased self-control. R&R
Prevention goals are strengthened.
Decrease chance of recidivism relapse.

Adapted with permission from G.H. Marlatt, 1985, Relapse Prevention: Theoretical rationale and overview. In G.A. Marlatt, & J.R.
Gordon (Eds.), Relapse Prevention: Maintenance Strategies in the treatment of addictive behaviors (p. 38), Guilford Press.

WORKSHEET 43

List some **high-risk thoughts** you have had **and/or high-risk situations** you have been in during the last few months that could have led to recidivism for you - either legal recidivism or "zero tolerance-zero risk" recidivism.

HIGH-RISK THINKING THAT CAN LEAD TO RECIDIVISM FOR YOU	HIGH-RISK SITUATIONS THAT CAN LEAD TO RECIDIVISM FOR YOU

WORKSHEET 44

List some **high-risk thoughts** you have had **and/or high-risk situations** you have been in during the last few months that could have led to relapse for you based on your personal relapse prevention

HIGH-RISK THINKING THAT CAN LEAD TO RELAPSE FOR YOU	HIGH-RISK SITUATIONS THAT CAN LEAD TO RELAPSE FOR YOU

Below are three triggers for relapse or recidivism. For each trigger, write in situations that apply to you. Then write your thoughts and feelings. What was the action you took? Did it lead to a positive or negative outcome? *Example:* You had a fight with your boss. Your thought, "screw the job." You felt angry. *Your action:* you went to talk with a friend, a positive coping behavior.

TRIGGERS	THOUGHTS	FEELINGS	ACTION
Unpleasant or negative feelings and emotions:			
Conflict with someone close or important to you:			
Social or peer pressure to drink or use drugs:			

Thinking and action skills that you have used in the past three to six months that have helped you prevent recidivism.

THINKING SKILLS YOU HAVE USED TO PREVENT RECIDIVISM	ACTION SKILLS YOU HAVE USED TO PREVENT RECIDIVISM

Thinking and action skills that you have used in the past three to six months that have helped you prevent relapse.

THINKING SKILLS YOU HAVE USED TO PREVENT RELAPSE	ACTION SKILLS YOU HAVE USED TO PREVENT RELAPSE

Thinking report: Use an event that was a high-risk situation for relapse or recidivism.

Describe the event:

Your thoughts:

Your feelings:

Your attitudes and beliefs:

The outcome:

SESSION 18

RELAPSE AND RECIDIVISM PREVENTION

YOUR RELAPSE AND RECIDIVISM

PREVENTION PLAN AND LIFESTYLE

BALANCE

INTRODUCTION AND SESSION OBJECTIVES

YOU HAVE DONE some good work on understanding relapse and recidivism (R&R) and on learning about R&R prevention. You have developed your recidivism and relapse prevention goals. You now have a good understanding of the R&R process, of risk thinking and high-risk exposures and the R&R prevention process. In this session we will work on strengthening your R&R prevention plan. This will involve having a clear idea of the *strategies you will use to stay on the R&R prevention path.* You will also look at the decisions you have made about your R&R prevention goals. We will look at developing and maintaining a *balanced lifestyle.*

OBJECTIVE FOR THIS SESSION

▶ Develop strategies to stay on the R&R prevention path.

▶ Look at the outcomes of your R&R prevention decisions.

▶ Develop a plan to maintain a lifestyle balance.

▶ Develop specific plans for potential R&R situations and thinking.

▶ Commit yourself to stay on the road of responsible living.

FIRST, WE WILL:

▶ do the CB MAP Exercise, having the event be a high-risk situation for impaired driving that a group member was faced with;

▶ discuss your AOD Weekly Monitoring Chart; and

▶ review and share your thinking report homework on high-risk event for relapse or recidivism.

SESSION CONTENT

A. RELATING YOUR RISK FOR RELAPSE AND RECIDIVISM TO YOUR MASTER PROFILE AND MASTER ASSESSMENT PLAN

You are much higher risk if you rated yourself high on these scales of your *Master Profile: frequency/quantity scales; gregarious drinking; AOD use to cope with social discomfort and with relationships; the negative consequence scales; and the impaired driving assessment scales.*

B. AS YOU WORK ON YOUR RELAPSE AND RECIDIVISM PREVENTION PLAN, REMEMBER HOW PEOPLE CHANGE AND THE STAGES OR STEPS OF CHANGE

▶ First, we are **challenged to change.** Getting your DWI was the beginning of this challenge. The **DWC** Education program challenged you to change. We did this by helping you become aware of your problems and the areas you need to change. Few people make changes unless they are challenged.

- The next step is the **commitment stage.** How do you know you are committed to change? When you openly talk about the patterns of AOD use that led to your DWI. When you come to these sessions with a positive attitude. When you continue to honor your personal and community commitment and not drive while impaired. When you have changed your thought and action habits that lead to DWI behavior.

- The third step is the **ownership stage.** You own the change. It belongs to you. How do you know you are taking ownership for your change? When you take full responsibility for your DWI offense. No excuses. No blame. You own the change when you take *personal responsibility* for making sure you do not drive while impaired. **When you come to this program because you want to, not because you have to.** When the goal to never drive when impaired becomes your goal and not just society's goal. When you are able to continue and maintain the changes you have made with confidence and self-control. You own your change when you do not drive impaired because you CARE about yourself, others and your community.

C. WORKING YOUR PLANS: STAYING ON THE RECIDIVISM AND RELAPSE PREVENTION PATH

In the last session, we worked on and practiced the skills to prevent relapse and recidivism. We looked at:

- The path leading to relapse and the path leading to recidivism, Figure 9, page 159; and
- The path leading to R&R prevention, Figure 10, page 160. We will now work on the specific high risk exposures in your life that can lead to R&R and specific skills you will use to prevent R&R.

Exercise: *Work Sheet 49,* page 173, provides these two paths. Complete the left side of the *Work Sheet* that describes your R&R pathway. Then, on the right side, put the skills that you will use to manage the high-risk exposures and stay on the path. How do you see your self-mastery of these skills? Do you own the changes you have made?

D. THE DECISION WINDOW

There are consequences for decisions. Your R&R prevention goals will have short-term outcomes and long-term outcomes. Many of these will be positive. Some may be negative. But take a realistic look at these outcomes.

Exercise: *Work Sheet 50,* page 174, provides the *decision windows.* Complete the windows for both alcohol and other drugs and for DWI recidivism.

- For the AOD decision window, put a check by the relapse prevention goal you have chosen: either living free of alcohol or other drugs; or the goal of living free of AOD problem outcomes.

- For the DWI recidivism window, put a check by your recidivism prevention goal: not to drive while impaired; or drive AOD free.

- Let's say you choose your relapse prevention goal of being AOD free. What do you get right now (short run) and later (long run) by not drinking or using drugs? What do you miss out on by not drinking, both in the short and long run?

- Do the same for the recidivism window. What do you get in the short and long run by being AOD free when driving? What do you miss out on by NOT driving impaired in the short and long run?

E. HOW LIFESTYLE IMBALANCES LEAD TO RELAPSE

You have made some important changes in your life. You have decided to abstain from AOD use or live free of AOD use problems. Maybe you have decided you will be AOD free every time you drive. This may be a very big change for you. But the demands of these changes may have caused some imbalances in your life. You may feel pressured, hassled and controlled. You may feel the pressure of the *shoulds or the oughts* to meet the demands of everyday living and the demands of staying on the narrow path towards your R&R prevention goals.

You are living free of AOD problems, not driving impaired, but because of these changes, you may feel somewhat cheated. You may not have the fun you used to have. You are more careful to avoid going to parties or at the bar and drinking because you don't want to drive impaired. You might be putting more time into your work, your family, and you think you have less time for yourself. You take your relapse and recidivism prevention goals serious. You are committed to these goals.

But because of this, life seems to be getting out of balance. This is a common experience for DWI offenders who make important changes in their AOD use patterns and their patterns of driving related to AOD use.

This imbalance might bring on a strong desire to meet the needs you gave up because of the changes you have made. As the desire increases, so does your need to get back to the old lifestyle that you had when you were drinking or using drugs with friends, going to the bar and parties, without the worry of drinking and driving impaired. There is the desire and maybe urges and cravings to drink and not worry about the consequences or outcomes. This makes your desire for the old lifestyle even stronger and to get back to the balance you had when you were drinking without worry. You may even begin to feel resentful and think:

▶ "I deserve more than this;"
▶ "I deserve a good time - a few drinks;" and
▶ "I have a right to drink with my friends."

This thinking and behavior can slowly lead to relapse and recidivism. A few drinks or going back to the old drinking patterns gives you immediate rewards. But it is gradual, like erosion. It sneaks up on you. You make small choices that don't seem important. You say, "I'll just go by the bar (where you spent a lot of time before your DWI arrest) and pick up something to go." We call this *Seemingly Irrelevant Decisions (SIDS)*. You may engage in high- risk thinking. You think: "I'll just have a coke or just one beer while I wait for my order to go." High-risk thinking and high-risk situation. These are all shown in the boxed parts of *Figure 11,* page 171.

Given all of this, how can you get your own needs met and still stay true to your R&R goals? You can do this by building a healthy balance between activities that cause you pressure and stress and activities that bring you pleasure and self-fulfillment.

F. **DEVELOPING A BALANCED LIFESTYLE - ADDING TO YOUR RELAPSE PREVENTION PLAN**

You worked on your relapse prevention plan in *Session 17.* That plan was based on the skills you would use to deal with high-risk thinking and high-risk situations. You did more work on that plan in Work Sheets 49 and 50 below. Now, we want you to add to that plan, a plan based on a balanced lifestyle. *Figure 11,* page 171, adds to your *relapse prevention plan* and provides you with a more balanced lifestyle. Fill in the circles.

1. **Positive involvements and replacing indulgences.**

   The circled parts of *Figure 11* give us general ways or strategies that help us handle the boxed parts of *Figure 11.* We can build a balanced lifestyle by building in daily activities that give us outcomes and rewards. When we feel a desire to spend time using alcohol or other drugs, we can put something else in its place. This means having positive involvements and **substituting** or replacing indulgences. We should be ready with those when we need them. These are activities that provide rather quick self-gratification (such as eating a nice meal, working in your woodshop, working on your car, cooking a meal, going for a hike, etc.).

2. **Detaching and labeling and ways to cope**

   We get the strong desire to go back to the old lifestyle, such as meeting friends at the bar, drink what you want and not worry. You want to have fun, drink 4 or 5 beers. *We call these cravings and urges. The urges and cravings may not only be for alcohol but for the lifestyle and pleasures that revolves around drinking.* We may get urges when we go into the bar for a "carry-out" and smell alcohol, or see people drink. The best way to cope with these is to **detach** or remove yourself from these high-risk situations. You can also put a **label** on the urge and desire, and then tell yourself, "ride it out." The urge does go away. You can use the coping skills you learned.

3. **Don't make excuses. Watch those decisions that don't seem important.**

   A powerful part of relapse is *making excuses,* to deny or defend against the cravings or need for the old lifesyle or get grunk now. You might think that the choices you make that move towards relapse or recidivism seem small - Seemingly Irrelevant Decisions (SIDS). Label these as warning signs. You think, "I deserve it." Label it "poor excuse." (PE). When you think this, it should warn you that you are moving towards relapse. You can also look at the short-term and long-term good and bad parts of a decision to not drink or not drink and drive. This is the decision window you worked on.

4. **Ways to avoid and cope with those high-risk situations that are steps to relapse and recidivism.**
   - ▶ Use what we call our community reinforcement groups to prevent relapse and recidivism - AA, NA, other twelve-step programs.
   - ▶ Think about volunteering time with a community agency.
   - ▶ Spend more time with your family, non-drinking friends.

5. **Exercise:** Complete the balanced lifestyle plan on *Figure 11.* Fill in the circles. Do this in group. Your counselor will help you.

G. YOUR HIGHWAY MAP FOR RESPONSIBLE LIVING

Your relapse and recidivism (R&R) prevention plan is a map for responsible living. *Figure 12,* page 172, shows a highway map for R&R or R&R prevention. You may have found yourself on a similar highway several times. You may have had chances to relapse and/or driving while impaired and were faced with one of two choices: continue on to The City of Responsible Living or to Collapse City. Our goal for you in this program is to help you stay on R & R Prevention 101 to Responsible City as shown on the map. What changes would you make to the map to fit your recidivism prevention goal on page 155 and your relapse prevention goal on page 156? Make the map to fit you. Write in the changes. It's your MAP to RESPONSIBLE LIVING. It is important to remember that if a person has moved towards collapse city, he or she has the choice at any time to backtrack and move up on the road to responsible or recovery city. Or, if you have found yourself in Collapse City, you can take Treatment Road 100 back to Prevention Road 101.

SESSION AND HOMEWORK ACTIVITIES

A. Update your Master Skills List and update your level of skills mastery, page 31.

B. Do your *AOD Weekly Monitoring Chart.*

C. During this coming week, look for high-risk exposures that could lead to relapse or recidivism.

CLOSURE PROCESS GROUP

Discuss how the highway map to the City of Responsible Living fits you.

FIGURE 11

Relapse and recidivism plan based on Lifestyle Balance

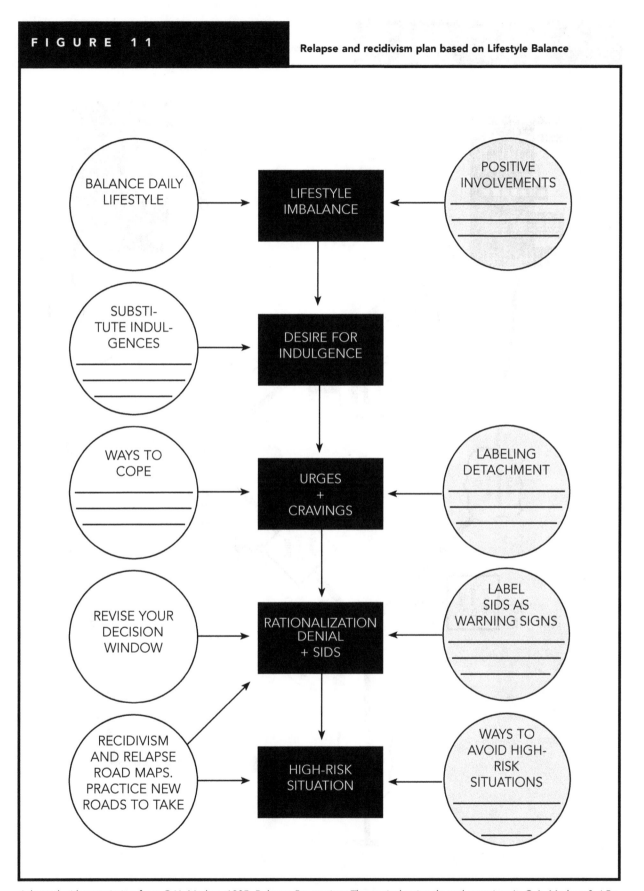

Adapted with permission from G.H. Marlatt, 1985, Relapse Prevention: Theoretical rationale and overview. In G.A. Marlatt, & J.R. Gordon (Eds.), Relapse Prevention: Maintenance Strategies in the treatment of addictive behaviors (p. 61), Guilford Press.

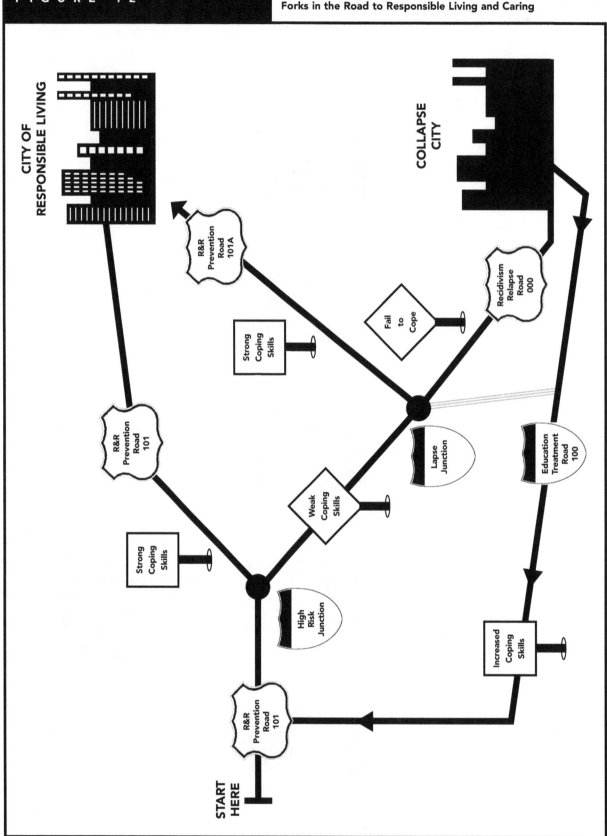

FIGURE 12

Forks in the Road to Responsible Living and Caring

Adapted with permission from authors G.A. Parks and G.H. Marlatt, 1999, Relapse Prevention therapy for Substance Abusing Offenders: A Cognitive-Behavioral Approach. In E. Latessa (Ed.), *What Works - Strategic Solutions: The International Community Corrections Association Examines Substance Abuse*, American Correctional Association.

R&R Prevention Skills: In the left column, describe your high-risk exposures, attitudes and beliefs that can lead to relapse and/or recidivism. Then, in the right column, describe the skills you will use to stay on the R&R prevention path.

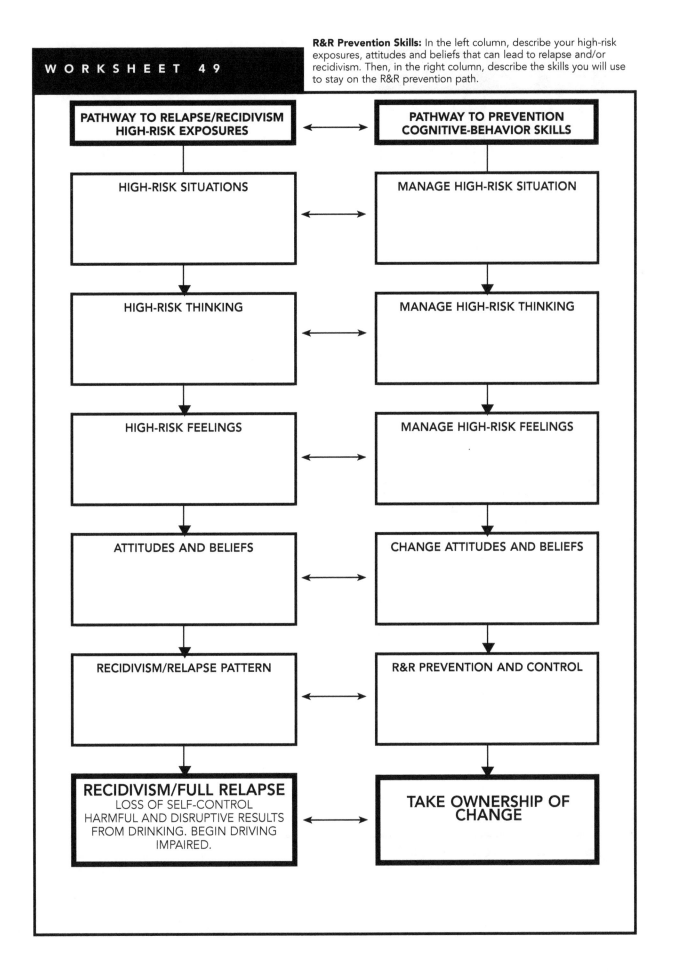

PATHWAY TO RELAPSE/RECIDIVISM HIGH-RISK EXPOSURES ⟷ **PATHWAY TO PREVENTION COGNITIVE-BEHAVIOR SKILLS**

HIGH-RISK SITUATIONS	MANAGE HIGH-RISK SITUATION
HIGH-RISK THINKING	MANAGE HIGH-RISK THINKING
HIGH-RISK FEELINGS	MANAGE HIGH-RISK FEELINGS
ATTITUDES AND BELIEFS	CHANGE ATTITUDES AND BELIEFS
RECIDIVISM/RELAPSE PATTERN	R&R PREVENTION AND CONTROL

RECIDIVISM/FULL RELAPSE
LOSS OF SELF-CONTROL HARMFUL AND DISRUPTIVE RESULTS FROM DRINKING. BEGIN DRIVING IMPAIRED.

TAKE OWNERSHIP OF CHANGE

WORKSHEET 50

Relapse Decision Window for AOD Use and Abuse Outcomes

YOUR RELAPSE PREVENTION GOAL:	IMMEDIATE OUTCOME (SHORT RUN)		DELAYED OUTCOME (LONG RUN)	
	POSITIVE	NEGATIVE	POSITIVE	NEGATIVE
❑ Living free of alcohol or other drugs (AOD) ❑ Living free of AOD problem outcomes				
CONTINUE TO USE AND ABUSE ALCOHOL AND OTHER DRUGS				

WORKSHEET 50

Recidivism Decision Window for impaired driving

YOUR RECIDIVISM PREVENTION GOAL:	IMMEDIATE OUTCOME (SHORT RUN)		DELAYED OUTCOME (LONG RUN)	
	POSITIVE	NEGATIVE	POSITIVE	NEGATIVE
❑ Drive AOD free ❑ Not drive while impaired				
CONTINUE TO DRIVE WHILE IMPAIRED				

Adapted with permission from G.H. Marlatt, 1985, Relapse Prevention: Theoretical rationale and overview. In G.A. Marlatt, & J.R. Gordon (Eds.), Relapse Prevention: Maintenance Strategies in the treatment of addictive behaviors (p. 58), Guilford Press.

SESSION 19

COMMUNITY RESPONSIBILITY SKILLS

STRENGTHENING CHARACTER AND PROSOCIAL VALUES AND BEHAVIOR

INTRODUCTION AND SESSION OBJECTIVES

THE NEXT THREE sessions will look at our responsibility to our community and society. Our focus on the skills of cognitive self-control and positive relationships with others is important in helping us relate to our community in a responsible way. Now, we will look at approaches for developing *responsible attitudes and behaviors in our community.*

Throughout **DWC Education** and **DWC Therapy,** we have been concerned about strengthening our *moral character* and *prosocial values.* We have worked on the values of;

▶ being concerned about and CARING for others; and
▶ building positive relationships with others and our community.

In **DWC Education,** we looked at our personal values and prosocial attitudes and behavior. This session will look at strengthening character and prosocial values and behavior.

OBJECTIVES FOR THIS SESSION
▶ See what antisocial behaviors and attitudes might fit you.
▶ Look at ways to strengthen moral character in order to increase responsible behavior in the community.

WE START THIS SESSION BY:
▶ Doing the CB MAP Exercise around an event that caused a craving;
▶ Review homework of looking for high-risk exposures that could have led to relapse or recidivism.

SESSION CONTENT AND FOCUS

A. WHAT GUIDES US IN RESPONSIBLE LIVING?

▶ Our personal values.
▶ Our personal morals.
▶ Following the standards of conduct and laws of your community.
▶ Being prosocial in relationship to others and our community.

Exercise: Group members will be asked to share some of their most important personal values and morals.

B. UNDERSTANDING PROSOCIAL, ANTISOCIAL AND MORAL CHARACTER

1. **Prosocial.** Involves a pattern of respecting the rights of others, complying with the norms, rules and laws of society and living in harmony with the community.

2. **Antisocial.** Involves a pattern of disregarding and violating the rights of others, doing harm to others and going against the rules and laws of society.

3. **Character.** The moral and ethical features of a person. For our purpose in this session, it means moral strength.

C. HOW DO YOU SEE YOURSELF? MORE ANTISOCIAL OR MORE PROSOCIAL?

1. **First, confront this fact:** DWI behavior involves going against the rules and laws of society.

2. **You may not see yourself as being antisocial, but your DWI conduct was antisocial behavior.**

3. **We now want you to take an honest look at your antisocial attitudes and behavior.**
   Exercise: *Work Sheet 51,* page 181, provides statements that would describe antisocial attitudes and behavior. The more "sometimes" and "much of the time" responses you have, the less likely you are to be prosocial and the more likely you are to be involved in antisocial behaviors and attitudes. The lower your score, the more you see yourself as prosocial. A very low score of 6 or less *suggests* you are being defensive about seeing yourself as antisocial. A score of around 7 to 15 *suggests* you have some antisocial attitudes and behaviors that could cause you problems. A score of around 16 to 25 *suggests* you have antisocial attitudes and behaviors that are causing problems in your life. A score above 25 suggests antisocial behaviors and attitudes that *may* be causing you a lot of problems — even serious ones — in your life.

4. **Practice changing your antisocial attitudes.**
   Exercise: Make a prosocial statement out of each statement in *Work Sheet 51.* Do it as a group in the Closure Process for this session.

5. **From your work on** *Work Sheet 51,* **rate yourself as to the need to change your antisocial attitudes and behaviors that you see yourself as having and to strengthen your prosocial attitudes, behaviors and moral character.** Check one of the following statements.

   ❑ I need to make a lot of changes in becoming more prosocial and strengthening my moral character.

   ❑ I need to make some changes in becoming more prosocial and strengthening my moral character.

   ❑ I need to make just a few changes in becoming more prosocial and strengthening my moral character.

   ❑ I do not need to make any changes. I am prosocial and have strong moral character.

   The less prosocial you are, the greater are your chances of taking part in future DWI behavior.

D. **SOME GUIDELINES AND SKILLS FOR STRENGTHENING MORAL CHARACTER AND PROSOCIAL ATTITUDES AND VALUES**

1. **Change the antisocial errors in thinking that can lead to antisocial actions.**
   Exercise: *Work Sheet 52,* page 182, gives you a list of antisocial thoughts and relationships that are errors in thinking. Check the errors you use. Practice changing the antisocial thoughts and relationships to prosocial thinking and prosocial relationships.

2. **Work at developing empathy or understanding of the position of other people - how they think and how they feel.** Use *active listening* to do this. We will work more on *empathy* next session.

3. **Remember that you are part of the whole of society.** When you hurt society, you hurt yourself. When you have an accident, not only do your insurance rates go up, but those of your children, your spouse, your parents. You may "slip on your own spills."

4. **Think about how your behavior affects other people, such as throwing a candy wrapper or cigarette butt on the street.** You become more prosocial and build character when you change these actions.

5. **You are a role model for others, for your children.** People watch you and copy you.

6. **Think of yourself as an important person.** Increase your self-esteem.

7. **Be part of the solution and not part of society's problem.**

8. **Think of yourself as a CARETAKER of your community, your society, the earth.**

9. **Do something each day that shows respect, consideration and kindness for others.**

   ‣ Hold the door for someone.
   ‣ Let someone change lanes in front of you.
   ‣ Hold the elevator door open for someone.
   ‣ Give someone a smile.
   ‣ Let people merge in traffic.

10. **Reach out to your community by volunteering your time to a charity, a church, an agency that serves people.**

E. THE MORAL DILEMMA

▶ The moral dilemma puts you in conflict with a value or moral that you hold and a rule that is placed on you by someone other than yourself. It could be two moral beliefs that are in conflict with each other. You are being prosocial when you hold to your morals and still stay in harmony with and responsible towards society. Discuss these in group.

- You value being loyal to friends. A close friend wants you to do something that is not legal.
- You have a moral value that you don't lend money to your friends. But a close friend desperately needs some money to pay his rent.

▶ Write down one moral dilemma you have faced in this past year. How did you resolve it?

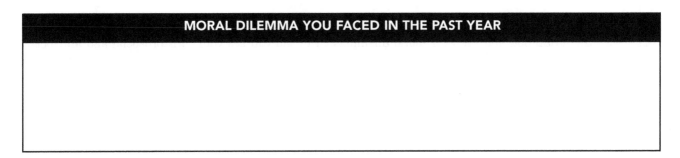

MORAL DILEMMA YOU FACED IN THE PAST YEAR

▶ **Exercise:** A security guard patrolling the grounds of General Hospital came across a man lying on the ground, a wound in his chest, and bleeding heavily. He had to have immediate medical attention. The guard ran into the hospital emergency room, where the only person he saw was an upset mother whose child appeared to have a broken arm. He found a nurse on duty and tried to get her to go help the man. The nurse said she could not leave the emergency room and all of the doctors were out. "This man will die if you don't help him," the guard insisted. The nurse pointed to a sign on the wall. "HOSPITAL EMPLOYEES MAY NOT LEAVE THE BUILDING WHEN ON DUTY." She wanted to help, but couldn't because of the rules.

Dilemma: Should she stay on duty or go help the wounded man? Discuss the dilemma in group. Take a position in this dilemma. Argue that position.

F. RELATING STRENGTHENING PROSOCIAL VALUES TO YOUR MASTER PROFILE AND MAP

▶ Look at Part III, Assessment of Thinking, Feeling and Attitude Patterns of your Master Profile (page 33). What parts of your MP results on page 33 fit with this session? Pick out the statements in your MP on page 33 that indicate antisocial thinking or attitudes.

▶ Do you need to add to your MAP based on what you learned from this session? Should you add antisocial attitudes and behaviors to your MAP as problems to work on?

SESSION ACTIVITIES AND HOMEWORK

A. Do Work Sheets 51 and 52.

B. Update your Master Skills List and skills ratings on page 31.

C. Do your AOD Monitoring Chart for this week.

CLOSURE PROCESS GROUP

Share with the group how you see your moral dilemmas. How do you see your own prosocial and antisocial features?

Antisocial behavior and attitudes: Rate yourself on these attitudes and behaviors that are seen as more antisocial and not prosocial. For every check in the "Ususally does not fit me" column, give yourself a "0." For every check in the "Fits me sometimes," give yourself a "1." For every check in the "Fits me much of the time," give yourself a "2."

ANTISOCIAL BEHAVIORS AND ATTITUDES	0 USUALLY DOES NOT FIT ME	1 FITS ME SOMETIMES	2 FITS ME MUCH OF THE TIME
1. Am impulsive and fail to plan ahead.			
2. Get aggressive and into physical fights.			
3. Get frustrated easily.			
4. Poor problem solving skills in relationships.			
5. Lack guilt and remorse when hurting others.			
6. Do not follow the rules.			
7. Do things that can get arrested for.			
8. Do not follow social norms.			
9. Lie or don't tell the truth.			
10. Con others for personal gain.			
11. Am reckless and not careful about my safety or safety of others.			
12. Not responsible with money/finances.			
13. Not responsible in relationships.			
14. Hard to put off a need when have it.			
15. Not responsible in work or job.			
16. Deny responsibility for own mistakes.			
17. Blame others for my mistakes.			
18. Have friends who take part in illegal actions or behaviors.			
19. Violate the rights of others.			
20. Lack understanding (empathy) for others.			
TOTAL SCORE			

Changing antisocial thinking errors and **social relationships** that can lead to antisocial behaviors and outcomes with thoughts and social relationships that can lead to prosocial behaviors and outcomes.

ERRORS IN THINKING OR SOCIAL RELATIONSHIPS THAT COULD LEAD TO ANTISOCIAL BEHAVIOR AND OUTCOMES.	REPLACE WITH PROSOCIAL THOUGHTS OR PROSOCIAL RELATIONSHIPS THAT LEAD TO PROSOCIAL BEHAVIORS/OUTCOMES.
POWER THRUST: "I'm better than others."	
INNOCENT: "I didn't know I was breaking the law."	
BLAMING STANCE: "It's your fault this happened to me."	
DOESN'T MATTER: "It's ok if it doesn't hurt anybody."	
VICTIM STANCE: "Somebody's always blaming me."	
CARELESS: "I don't care how it affects somebody else."	
JUST DESERTS: "They had it coming."	
DISTRUST: "You can't trust anybody."	
CHEATED: "I never get what's coming to me."	
SCREWED: "I'm always getting screwed."	
SOCIAL: Spending a lot of time with antisocial friends.	
RELATIONSHIP: Rejecting family or friends who are supportive.	
SOCIAL: Always critical or angry at people.	
SOCIAL: Spending all free time in bar drinking.	
SOCIAL: Most friends are angry at society and laws of society.	

SESSION 20

COMMUNITY RESPONSIBILITY SKILLS

UNDERSTANDING AND PRACTICING EMPATHY

INTRODUCTION AND SESSION OBJECTIVES

VALUES AND MORALS differ across all peoples and nations. Yet, there are laws across all communities and cultures that have one thing in common: the safety and welfare of people. Basic to this concern for others is what we call *empathy*. An important part of self-control is *empathy - being sensitive to the suffering and plight of others and putting oneself in the place of others*. Empathy is one of the most important parts of moral character, prosocial behavior and responsibility towards the community. Responsible living is considering the attitudes, feelings and views of others - becoming more understanding towards and caring of others.

Why is this topic important for you? First, alcohol and other drug use can prevent people from having an understanding of other people - or can prevent us from putting ourselves in the position of others. Second, AOD problem outcomes most often hurt other people. Part of preventing relapse and changing AOD problem use patterns is having empathy for those who are hurt by these patterns. Third, when we engage in DWI behavior, we show a *lack of empathy*. Impaired drivers have difficulty putting themselves in the "shoes of other drivers." They fail to understand the danger they place others and themselves in. Having empathy for others is a cornerstone for preventing recidivism into impaired driving.

We began to practice having empathy in our last session through the *moral dilemma* - or situations in which our ideas clash with those of other people. It helped us understand the position of other people as we followed our own moral beliefs.

OBJECTIVES FOR THIS SESSION
- Understand the difference between sympathy and empathy.
- Learn to consider the position of other people - learn empathy.
- Understand how empathy is the basis of prosocial behavior and attitudes.

WE START THIS SESSION DOING THE FOLLOWING:

- AOD MAP Exercise, using an event where you saw someone behave or act in an antisocial way.
- Review your AOD Weekly Monitoring Chart
- Update your MAP. Do you need to put dates on completing some of the problems? Do you need to add new problems?

SESSION CONTENT AND FOCUS

A. SYMPATHY AND EMPATHY: THEY ARE BOTH IMPORTANT IN CARING ABOUT OTHERS AND IN RESPONSIBLE LIVING

1. What is sympathy?

▶ Sympathy is an emotional response to something outside of ourselves.

▶ It is feeling sorry or having pity for another person or another living object.

▶ It is having compassion and feeling the pain or hurt of another person.

▶ It involves awareness of another person's pain.

▶ Sympathy does not have to involve understanding someone's pain. It does not involve the knowledge of the other person's pain.

▶ Sympathy is "your pain, my heart."

▶ Sympathy takes place after the fact — after you are aware of or see someone's hurt and pain.

2. What is empathy?

▶ Empathy is more than feeling the other person's pain and more than just emotional. It is having knowledge and understanding of that pain.

▶ Empathy is "your pain, my heart **and** head."

▶ It is putting ourselves in the place of the other person, particularly people we may have hurt or who have been victims of our actions.

▶ But empathy can take place before the fact before someone is in pain.

  • It is understanding pain someone can have.

  • It prevents us from actions that can hurt others. Empathy helps us visualize how our actions can affect others.

▶ Empathy is understanding, not just pain, but another person's hopes, thoughts, feelings, attitudes and beliefs.

▶ It is being sensitive to and concerned about others.

▶ When we have empathy for another person, we are able to:

  • relate to or know another person's feelings, motives, ideals or situation;

  • feel and have concern for another person; and

  • feel and understand another person's pain and suffering.

WHEN WE ARE ABLE TO PUT OURSELVES IN THE PLACE OF THE OTHER PERSON - WE ARE TRULY ABLE TO "WALK IN THE SHOES" OF THE OTHER PERSON.

B. PRACTICE HAVING EMPATHY OR FEELING EMPATHIC

When you use the reflection or "stating the other person's position" skill of active listening, you are practicing empathy.

Exercise: *Work Sheet 53*, page 187, gives four stories about something that happened to another person. Read each story and then put yourself in the place of that person. Close your eyes when you do this and really understand and feel what the person in that story went through. Then note in the second column what you think the other person was thinking and feeling.

Exercise: Break into small groups. Using the front sections of newspapers, pick one or two stories and then practice making empathic statements about the persons in the stories.

Exercise: In your small group and using the same newspapers, find a story that describes a *moral dilemma.* Complete *Work Sheet 54,* page 188, and then discuss what you wrote with the group.

C. RELATING IDEAS OF EMPATHY TO YOUR MASTER PROFILE AND MASTER ASSESSMENT PLAN

Look at your ratings in the *Impaired Driving Assessment* section of your MP, page 33. How do these ratings relate to the ideas of empathy? Look at your *Marital-Family Problems Scale* in the *Current Life Situation Problems Section* of your MP, page 34. Can you apply the ideas of empathy to your intimate partner relationship or to your family?

SESSION OR HOMEWORK ACTIVITIES

A. Use *Work Sheet 55,* page 189, and do a *Thinking Report.* Choose a situation where you had empathy for someone. Describe the situation, your thoughts and feelings. What beliefs must you have to support thoughts of empathy?

B. This may be difficult for you, but we are asking you to try it. Using the space on page 189 and 190, write a letter to a person who was affected by your DWI arrest episode. It can be a person who was hurt emotionally or physically. State what the person felt and experienced. This will help you feel concern and empathy for the people affected by your DWI offense. This letter is for you only. It is not to be mailed. To assure confidentiality, do not put the person's real name on the letter.

C. Update your Master Skills List and update your level of mastery for the skills you have worked on, page 31. Are you improving on the skills you have learned?

D. Do your *AOD Weekly Monitoring Chart.*

CLOSURE PROCESS GROUP

Discuss in group whether you have difficulty having empathy for other people. Empathy gives us self-control. Self-control leads to positive outcmes.

WORKSHEET 53

BELOW ARE FOUR STORIES. EACH STORY IS ABOUT A PARTICULAR INDIVIDUAL WHO HAS EXPERIENCED SOMETHING OF GREAT IMPORTANCE IN HIS OR HER LIFE. READ EACH STORY CAREFULLY.	PUT YOURSELF IN THE PLACE OF THE PERSON IN THE STORY. THEN WRITE DOWN WHAT YOU THINK THE OTHER PERSON WAS THINKING AND FEELING.
John is nine years old. He was hit by a car and was in the hospital for two months. He lost his right leg in the accident. He loved baseball, and was a very good player, he was feeling a great deal of sadness because he knew he would never play baseball again.	
Marie, who is 45 years old, struggled all of her life to make a living and support her family of four children. Her husband died just after the youngest was born. She works as a cook in a high school. Her oldest son is very smart and will be finishing high school this year. He wants to be a doctor, but Marie knows she does not and never will have the money to send him to college. The other day her son came home and told her that he received a full four year scholarship to attend college.	
Hank, age 30, a house framer and carpenter, was leaving work when a robber hit him on the head and stole his car. The robber stole his car and then drove over Hank when getting away. Hank has been in the hospital for two months. He has severe spinal injuries and will have to be in rehab for many months, and he may never walk again.	
Karen is 48, has six children and does not work outside of the house. Her husband drives a city bus. Yesterday she bought a lottery ticket. She and her husband checked the numbers today and found that they won a million dollars.	

Moral Dilemma. Find a newspaper article that presents a moral dilemma to the people involved.

1. DESCRIBE THE SITUATION.

2. WHO WAS THE CENTRAL CHARACTER IN THE EVENT?

3. WHY DO YOU BELIEVE THIS IS A MORAL DILEMMA?

4. WHAT SHOULD HAVE BEEN DONE IN THE SITUATION?

Thinking report: Choose a situation in which you have empathy for another person.

Describe the event:
Your thoughts:
Your feelings:
Your attitudes and beliefs:
The outcome:

LETTER TO SOMEONE AFFECTED BY YOUR DWI ARREST.

_____

_____

_____

_____

_____

_____

_____

SESSION 21

COMMUNITY RESPONSIBILITY
AND RELATIONSHIP SKILLS

RESOLVING CONFLICTS AND
NEGOTIATION SKILL DEVELOPMENT

INTRODUCTION AND SESSION OBJECTIVES

AN IMPORTANT PART OF this program has been that of working on developing attitudes and skills to improve our relationship with the community. The social and interpersonal skills that we learned - communication skills, problem solving, responsibility in intimate relationships - also help us to become more responsible members of the community.

In this session, we will look at some important ideas about *conflict and resolving conflicts.* This will help us in our social and interpersonal relationships as well as in our relationship with the community. Research has shown that persons with a history of AOD problems are less apt to relapse if they have mastered skills in managing their stress and emotions and their relationship with others. We call this *self-efficacy* or *self-mastery.* Persons who have *high self-efficacy* or *self-mastery* are less apt to return to AOD problem use and DWI behavior. An important area of self-mastery is resolving conflicts.

You may be thinking, "I don't have conflicts with other people!" But think about this. Your DWI put you in direct conflict with your community. You are doing many things to resolve this conflict. One of those is being in this program. Resolving conflicts means that sometimes you have to meet obligations; to be responsible to others and to the community. Are you resolving your conflict in a responsible way? The fact that you have been attending this program means that you are doing just that. THE FIRST STEP TO RESOLVING ANY CONFLICT IS TO TAKE RESPONSIBILITY FOR YOUR ROLE IN THE CONFLICT.

OBJECTIVES OF THIS SESSION

▶ Learn that resolving conflicts in a positive manner contributes to positive relationships with others and with the community.

▶ Learn that an open-minded approach to conflict is the best way to solve problems.

▶ Learn how to achieve a win-win solution in resolving conflicts.

▶ Learn to identify problems and develop new skills to solve them.

WE WILL START THIS SESSION BY:

▶ Doing the CB MAP Exercise, using an event related to empathy;

▶ Update your MAP;

▶ Briefly report your progress or your AOD Weekly Monitoring;

▶ Share the thinking report you did last session on empathy, Worksheet 55, page 189; and

▶ Have some members, who feel comfortable doing so, share their thoughts and feelings about the letter they wrote to someone affected by their DWI arrest and conviction.

SESSION CONTENT AND FOCUS

IT IS ALMOST impossible to live without conflict with others. You may find yourself in conflict because of the *changes you have made in your beliefs and actions* in this program. You may find yourself in conflict because you are now standing up for what you believe, which will make you a better person. Conflict with others can lead to stress, feelings of defeat and a lack of self-control. Conflict can test your relapse prevention goal and your goal of living in harmony with others and the community.

Most conflicts are solved by someone being right and someone being wrong. This is what we call adversarial or the *going to court* approach. This is the most common way that couples settle their disputes.

This program takes the approach that we should settle conflicts and solve problems so that you and the other person(s) or your community feel good about the outcome. This is what we call a win-win solution. You feel more of a master of your own life and your own changes when you settle conflicts so that you don't lose and the other person doesn't lose - a *win-win* outcome.

A. THE FOLLOWING ARE IMPORTANT PARTS OF CONFLICT OR PROBLEMS

- The make-up of the conflict or the situation and persons involved.
- The idea or what the conflict is about.
- The give-and-take of the conflict or what happens among those involved.

B. SOME IMPORTANT THINGS TO REMEMBER WHEN WORKING OUT A CONFLICT

- Everyone experiences or views the world from their own point of view and that the attitudes, values and beliefs of others should be respected.
- Solving conflicts does not require someone being wrong and someone being right.
- There is no one truth in most cases. Each person holds his or her own truths.
- Two people can both be partly right.
- Be part of the solution, not part of the problem.
- Keep your attention on the problem, not the person.
- Always work towards a *win-win* outcome.
- **Take responsibility for your part of the problem and your part of the solution.**

C. AVOID THE OLD WAYS YOU HAVE USED TO DEAL WITH CONFLICT

- FIGHT: becoming aggressive and forceful to get your way, which only increases the conflict or friction.
- FLIGHT: withdrawing or removing yourself from the conflict or friction and nothing is resolved.
- FAKE: going along with the other person but then do what you want anyway.

Instead, use the assertive or FAIR approach when dealing with conflicts.

D. WORKING FOR A WIN-WIN OUTCOME

Here are some skills you can use to get a good outcome and to reach an agreement around a conflict or problem. These are the skills of *negotiation* and *bargaining* with the goal of reaching a *win-win* outcome - everyone gains, no one loses completely.

1. **State your position,** your thoughts, feelings and goals and ideas - sharing your story.

2. **You ask the other persons involved about their thoughts, feelings, goals and ideas** - inviting the person to share.

3. **You state their position or tell them what you hear them saying - reflecting.**

4. **You then explain why you think your solution is the best solution** - give some evidence.

5. **You find out why they think their solution is better** - hear their evidence.

6. **Decide what you both agree on and put those aside.**

7. **Clearly spell out what you disagree on and both sides decide what each needs to get a solution.**

8. **You decide what you can give up and still feel you have won.** The other side decides what they can give up and still feel they have won. Make sure what you are holding onto is absolutely necessary. The other side does the same.

9. **Now look at what you have won.** Is it enough? Does the other side feel what they have won is enough? Make a decision: can you live with what you have won? Does it outweigh what you have given up? In most cases, the conflict is resolved.

If you are unable to agree at step nine, then you may have to have an outside party settle the matter. This is called **arbitration.**

E. HERE ARE THE SIMPLE STEPS OF NEGOTIATION

1. **STATE-ASK:** Tell the other person your position. Ask for the other person's opinion.

2. **LISTEN-REFLECT:** make sure you understand the other person's position. Reflect the other person's position to be sure you understand. Be open minded. Listen to the feedback.

3. **COMPARE-CONTRAST:** What do you agree on? Where do you differ? What are the options that might work? What won't work?

4. **OFFER-COMPROMISE:** Offer solutions. Ask the other person for solutions. Are they *win-win* solutions? Compromise to get a win-win and discuss the options.

5. **CHOOSE-AGREE:** decide which is best.

F. A GUIDE FOR DIAGNOSING HOW YOU APPROACH A CONFLICT

Dr. Reinhold Niebuhr wrote a prayer that has become known as the serenity prayer of Alcoholics Anonymous.

> God, grant me the serenity to accept the things I cannot change,
>
> The courage to change the things I can,
>
> And the wisdom to know the difference.

Make an effort to clearly understand each conflict that you may be a part of. Ask yourself: Can I change the situation or negotiate a settlement? Or, is it impossible to change what exists? If you decide that change and settlement are possible, then negotiate with strength and courage. If you truly see that change is not possible and there is no hope for negotiation, then accept what is with serenity and patience. Use your best wisdom and intelligence to know the difference. **Remember: Take responsibility for your role in the problem or conflict and in the solution.**

G. **EXERCISE:** USE *WORK SHEET 56,* **PAGE 196 TO DESCRIBE A CONFLICT YOU HAD IN WHICH YOU PRACTICED THE SKILLS OUTLINED ABOVE**

GROUP HOMEWORK AND ACTIVITIES

A. Update your Master Skills list, page 31. Add date to negotiations skills. Update your level of skill mastery for the skills you have learned.

B. Do your *AOD Weekly Monitoring Chart.*

C. Apply the skills you learned in this session to a conflict or problem you have this coming week.

CLOSURE PROCESS GROUP

Share with the group some conflicts that you are having in your life. Ask the group for help in solving these conflicts.

Negotiating Skills: Working for a Win-Win outcome. Describe a CONFLICT SITUATION which you were recently in and apply the following steps.

1. What did you want in order to resolve the conflict?

2. What did the other person want?

3. What were the options or different ways to solve the conflict?

4. What did you give to resolve the conflict?

5. What did the other person give?

6. What was the outcome? Was it win-win, lose-lose?

EXTENDED LEVEL II THERAPY

REFLECTION AND REVIEW AND

YOUR THERAPY PROJECTS

OVERVIEW

CONGRATULATIONS ON completing the 21 sessions of the DWC Therapy. We called this Track A of DWC Therapy. Some clients may be required to take additional therapy sessions beyond the DWC core 21 sessions. Thus, we have developed extended therapy sessions for this purpose. We have set up the extended therapy program in three additional tracks - B, C, and D. Although your specific program may not exactly fit these tracks, they will provide for you a program structure that can help you meet your required additional therapy.

You will share a *Reflection and Review Session* with your counselor to plan the treatment path you will take to complete your **DWC Therapy** program. You are asked to select therapy projects to work on in this extended part of **DWC Therapy.**

The Track B program involves completing the core 21 DWC Therapy program plus an additional ten hours of **DWC Therapy.** During your therapy, you are asked to select *two manual-guided therapy projects* to work on and present those in the group to which you are assigned. You will be given about 15 minutes to present your project to your group. You will also continue your *AOD Weekly Monitoring Chart.*

The Track C program involves 26 hours of therapy beyond the core 21 session DWC Therapy program. Clients are asked to complete *four manual-guided therapy projects* and present them to their group and continue the *AOD Weekly Monitoring Chart.*

The *Track D* program involves the core 21 session *DWC Therapy* program, an additional 44 hours of therapy, *eight manual-guided therapy projects* and continue the *AOD Weekly Monitoring Chart.* There are *10 manual-guided therapy projects* in your *Participant's Workbook* from which you may select your therapy projects. You may select a topic other than the 10 provided, if you feel there is an important area you need to work on.

OBJECTIVES OF EXTENDED LEVEL II THERAPY

IN THE 21 SESSION DWC core **Therapy** program, we learned and practiced the skills of mental self-control, relationship building and responsible community living.

The overall goal of extended **DWC Level II Therapy** is to prevent recidivism and relapse by giving you a longer period of therapy support in which to strengthen the changes made and practice and apply the knowledge and skills learned in the 21 Session DWC core therapy program. Here are the objectives of extended **Level II Therapy.**

▶ Look more deeply at specific life problems that can lead to relapse and recidivism.
▶ Further work on your recidivism and relapse prevention and lifestyle balance plan.
▶ Continue to practice the cognitive-behavioral (CB) approach to changing thinking, beliefs and attitudes.

- Strengthen the skills of cognitive self-control, managing relationships and trustworthy behavior in the community.
- Work on areas that are special to your own needs and concerns.
- Continue to work on responsible living and change that will lead to positive outcomes for yourself, for others and for your community.
- Find greater meaning and joy in your life!

REFLECTION AND REVIEW SESSION

Before starting the extended **DWC Therapy** program, you will meet with your counselor for a short reflection session to review and update your individual treatment plan and be assigned to one of the options below.

OBJECTIVES FOR THIS SESSION
- Review the progress you have made.
- Look at the areas you will work on during your extended **Therapy.**
- Select the therapy projects you will work on.
- Decide on the specific therapy path you will take to complete **your Therapy** based on your Individual Treatment Plan (ITP).

Some counselors or agencies may have a separate and open group for extended therapy clients and use the 10 therapy projects as therapy sessions. In this case you will be assigned to that open group. If not, here are some other options.

Option One. Complete your extended **Therapy** by staying in the Track A DWC core **Therapy** program as a *Peer Support Client.* Here is how you could do this.

- Repeat the number of DWC **Level II Therapy** sessions that meet your extended therapy requirements. If you are in *Track B,* you would repeat five **Level II Therapy** sessions.
- Help other clients in the group understand the sessions and complete the *Work Sheets*.
- Share with group members how you applied what you learned in these sessions to your life.
- Present your Therapy Project to the group.
- Receive special therapy based on your ITP.

As a *Peer Support Client,* you would not only help yourself but others who are in the 21 session DWC **Therapy** *Track A* program.

Option Two. You and your counselor could develop an individual program that is tailored to your needs. This could include:

▶ individual counseling;

▶ marital counseling;

▶ specialized groups such as stress management, anger management, etc;

▶ presentation of your therapy project in your group or in your individual session; or

▶ spending some sessions as a peer support client in a *Track A* **Therapy** Group.

Option Three. You would be assigned to a group in your agency such as a relapse and recidivism prevention group, a marital couples group, an aftercare group, or some other therapy group in your agency. Then you would attend the number of sessions in that group according to the number of extended therapy sessions you are required to complete.

▶ This assignment would be based on specific needs that you have.

▶ You would present your *Therapy Project* in that group.

YOUR STAGE OF CHANGE

REMEMBER WE TALKED about the stages people go through when they make changes. First, you were challenged to change when you were arrested for impaired driving. You met that challenge when you completed **DWC Education.** During **DWC Education,** you committed yourself to making changes so as to prevent recidivism and relapse. **DWC Therapy** was set up to help you continue your commitment to change and to take ownership of your changes. As part of this ownership step, we want you to make alternative lifestyle changes so as to build and maintain a healthy and balanced lifestyle.

THERAPY PROJECT 1: Healthy Play and Leisure Time

INTRODUCTION AND PROJECT OBJECTIVES

For many of you, involvement in drinking or using other drugs has been a main part of your lifestyle. If you have changed your AOD use pattern, and made AOD use a much less important part of your life, or not even part of your life, you may be restless or feeling somewhat lonely and empty because of the time you did spend in your AOD use. Unless you replace that void with some pleasant activities, there is a greater chance that you will relapse back to the old AOD use patterns. In maintaining an AOD problem-free life and to avoid recidivism, the alternative of healthy play and leisure time can be important. Here is what we want you to do in this project.

OBJECTIVES FOR THERAPY PROJECT 1

▶ Understanding the meaning of play.

▶ Learn about the activities that bring you the most pleasure.

▶ Discover that you have replaced activities involving alcohol and other drug use with healthy activities not involving AOD use.

▶ Learn how you can plan and fulfill healthy pleasures through leisure time activities that become a regular part of your life.

THERAPY PROJECT CONTENT AND ACTIVITIES

A. WHAT IS HEALTHY PLAY?

Play means to take part in fun, to have pleasure, to be amused, to enjoy an activity or to take part in a recreation. An important part of play is to **move freely within a space.** But the lifestyle alternative we are referring to is more than just play. It is healthy play. Healthy play means:

▶ you set limits on or structure your play as to time, cost, how much energy you put out;

▶ it is wholesome or moral;

▶ it is of benefit to you and to others;

▶ when you have finished taking part in play and leisure time, you will feel good about yourself;

▶ healthy play replaces unhealthy activities such as AOD use patterns that cause harm to you, others and your community; and most important

▶ healthy play always involves being responsible to others and to your community.

B. WHAT ARE THE ACTIVITIES THAT GIVE YOU PLEASURE AND ARE HEALTHY PLAY?

▶ The number of pleasant activities you take part in is related to how positive you feel about yourself. People who spend all their time doing required activities, the "shoulds" and "oughts," may experience little reward in life and are likely to feel they deserve to reward themselves with a drink, a hit, or a night out with friends that can lead to relapse.

▶ One way to learn healthy play is to *know what pleases you* or to know your pleasures. If you know what pleases you or what activities that give you pleasure, you will know how to play and your play will be more fulfilling.

▶ **Exercise:** Use *Work Sheet 57,* page 203, and make a list of activities that give you pleasure and joy and that are seen as healthy play. In the second column, write down how many times a month you do these activities. Do they help give you a balanced lifestyle?. In column 3, check if they are now replacements or alternatives to drinking or using other drugs. There are probably more lines in Worksheet 57 than you need. As you continue in **DWC Therapy,** add to the list new activities you get involved in.

C. PLANNING PERSONAL TIME FOR THESE HEALTHY PLAY ACTIVITIES

▶ **Exercise:** Using *Work Sheet 58,* page 204, list play and fun activities that you will take part in this week. Then, using the bottom part of *Work Sheet 58,* make a personal time schedule, and plan what your activity will be in that schedule. This will help you develop a balance in life between work and healthy play.

▶ What kind of problems are you having in finding alternative ways to fill your time? Have you been successful in finding new friends and acquaintances with whom to share leisure time?

HOMEWORK AND PRESENTING YOUR THERAPY PROJECT IN YOUR GROUP

A. Present this **Therapy Project** to your group. Have group members share activities that they find joy and pleasure in. If there is time, have group members do Work Sheets 57 and 58.

B. **Reflection and Review:** How are you doing in the program? Are you meeting your recidivism and relapse prevention goals?

C. Remember to do your *AOD Weekly Monitoring Chart.*

D. Continue to update the ratings on your Master Skills List, page 31.

NOTES

_____

_____

_____

_____

_____

_____

_____

_____

_____

_____

_____

Fun and play activities that you enjoy most. List the healthy leisure time and play activities that you most enjoy. In the second column, write down how many times a month you do these activities. In the third column, check if that activity has replaced drinking alcohol and/or using other drugs.

LEISURE TIME ACTIVITY	TIMES A MONTH	REPLACES AOD USE ACTIVITIES

Planning your leisure time activities.

FIRST, WRITE DOWN SEVERAL PLEASANT ACTIVITIES THAT YOU BELIEVE YOU WOULD ENJOY DOING IN THE NEXT WEEK.

On the chart below, plan 30 to 60 minutes each day for yourself. When the time comes, decide which of the things from the above list you want to do and take time to do it. Write down what you did and what you thought and felt about doing these things for yourself.

PERSONAL TIME	ACTIVITY YOU DID AND YOUR THOUGHTS ABOUT IT
MONDAY	
TUESDAY	
WEDNESDAY	
THURSDAY	
FRIDAY	
SATURDAY	
SUNDAY	

THERAPY PROJECT 2: Does Your Work Match Your Job?

INTRODUCTION

There is a difference between your work and your job. Your work is a physical or mental activity and effort that is directed towards accomplishing something. Your work is the means through which you practice your skills, fulfill your talents and earn your livelihood. Your job is what you go to in order to fulfill your work. You take your work to your job. You own your work. It is yours. You don't own your job; it is given to you in order to do your work. Work is one way you define your lifestyle.

OBJECTIVES FOR THERAPY PROJECT 2

▶ Learn what your work is or what is your area of work.

▶ Learn skills necessary to take part in rewarding work.

▶ Look at your education and work goals for the next three years.

THERAPY PROJECT CONTENT AND ACTIVITIES

A. WHAT IS YOUR WORK?

Use *Work Sheet 59,* page 207, to identify your work. Give a name to the work you do. Write down as many things as you can that defines your work. For example, a person may write down: Truck Driver. What is involved in that work? Being safe? Listening to the sounds of the truck as it is running? Driving the speed limit? Being on time for a delivery? Maintaining the vehicle? etc. In the second column, put a check for each of the statements that you like doing. If you check most of the items, then you like your work. Now, feel a sense of pride in your work. You may not like your job; but you can love your work. Feel power in that.

If you check that you like only a few things about your work, then you may not like your work. You may need to look for another kind of work. Do you need to get training in another line of work? Talk this over with your counselor. You may want to go into a program of looking at your vocational or work interests.

B. DOES YOUR JOB MATCH YOUR WORK?

You may like your work, but does your work fit your job? See if your job matches your work. In the right column of *Work Sheet 59,* check each item that matches the job you now have. If you check most of the statements, then your job matches your work. If not, you may not be happy in the job you have. You may want to look for a different job that better matches your work.

C. DO YOU NEED TO LOOK FOR A JOB?

If you do not have a job or if your job does not match your work and you are not happy in your job, you may want to do a job search. *Therapy Project 3* will help you in this.

HOMEWORK AND PRESENTING YOUR THERAPY PROJECT IN YOUR GROUP

A. Present this **Therapy Project** to the group you are now in. Share what you got out of it. Ask the group members to share their work and whether their work matches their job.

B. **Reflection and Review:** How are you doing in the program at this time? Are you meeting your recidivism and relapse prevention goals?

C. Do your *AOD Weekly Monitoring Chart.*

D. Review your *Master Assessment Plan.* Do you need special help in working on some of your problems?

E. Update your Master Skills ratings, page 31.

NOTES

_____

_____

_____

_____

_____

_____

_____

_____

_____

_____

_____

What is your work? First, give a name to your work. The following are some examples: Truck Driver, Tile Setter, Bookkeeper, Sales Person, etc. Then, write down everything you think of that defines your work or the important parts of your work. Use extra paper if you run out of room in this Work Sheet.

NAME OF MY WORK

List what defines your work or the important parts of your work.	Check if like doing this	Check if matches your job

THERAPY PROJECT 3: Learning to Search for a Job

INTRODUCTION

In *Therapy Project 2,* we looked at whether you like your work and whether your work matches your job. Do you need to look for another job? Do you need to learn work skills you feel more satisfied with? Do you have a job?

OBJECTIVES FOR THERAPY PROJECT 3

▶ Learn skills to look for a job;

▶ Look at your education and work goals for the next three years.

THERAPY PROJECT ACTIVITIES

A. STEPS IN LOOKING FOR A JOB

▶ **Developing a Résumé** that describes your work history and desire for work. Explain periods of time that you were not working. The document should be carefully typed and include a cover letter.

▶ **The Job Application:** The job applicant needs to be able to emphasize personal strengths and strong job skills.

▶ **Job Leads:** *Using Work Sheet 60,* page 209, make a list of 10 possible jobs and employers. Job seeking is a full-time job. Go after each one until you succeed.

▶ **Develop Telephone Skills:** Introduce yourself and ask to speak to the person in charge of hiring. Set up an appointment. Practice your *phone skills.*

▶ **The Interview:** *Practice job interviewing.* Be prepared for success and failure. You own your work, so sell it. You can't buy the job but you can sell your work. Role play a job interview in your group.

▶ **Set Goals:** What are your short-term goals? What are your long-term goals? Look at your plan for school and/or work for the next three years. Use *Work Sheet 61,* page 210.

HOMEWORK AND PRESENTING YOUR THERAPY PROJECT IN YOUR GROUP

A. Present this **Therapy Project** to your group. Ask the group members to share. Do Work Sheets 60 and 61.

B. **Reflection and Review:** How are you doing in the program? Are you meeting your R&R prevention goals?

C. Do your *AOD Weekly Monitoring Chart.*

D. Update your Master Skills Ratings, page 31.

Job Search Plan. Make a list of 10 possible jobs including the names of companies, address, phone number, and what happened to you when you made the call.

NAME OF JOB	NAME OF EMPLOYER	DATE CONTACTED	CONTACT NAMES AND NUMBERS	NOTES

School and Work Plan for the Next Three Years. List your specific objectives for education, schooling and work for the next three years. Share this with your group.

LIST SPECIFIC OBJECTIVES IN SCHOOL AND WORK PLAN FOR THE NEXT 3 YEARS

THERAPY PROJECT 4: Learning to Relax: Your Daily Relaxation Plan

INTRODUCTION

In **DWC Therapy**, you learned skills in managing stress. We looked at how to change your thinking to manage stress and the emotions of anger, guilt and depression related to stress. In this Session, we learn strategies that **prepare** us for stress and to handle the stress syndromes of anger, guilt and depression.

OBJECTIVES FOR THERAPY PROJECT 4
▶ Learn relaxation strategies and methods
▶ Develop a weekly relaxation plan.

THERAPY PROJECT CONTENT AND ACTIVITIES

A. REVIEW SESSION 8, PAGE 79 AND THE STEPS OF MANAGING STRESS

B. THERE ARE TWO STRATEGIES IN MANAGING STRESS

▶ *Handling* stressful events as they come up. This was the topic of *Session 8,* page 79.
▶ *Preparing* for stressful events. An athlete trains each day to play a game. When game time comes - the time of stress - he or she is ready to play. The same is true with preparing for stressful events. In this *Therapy Project,* we will learn relaxation strategies that prepare us for stress.

C. HERE IS WHAT RELAXATION DOES

▶ Stops the negative results of stress.
▶ Lets tension flow from our minds and body.
▶ Gives you relaxed thoughts.
▶ Gives you energy.
▶ Prepares you for handling stressful events and to use the skills to manage those events.
▶ Brings body and mind together as one.

D. DAILY RELAXATION STRATEGIES

▶ **Mental relaxation.**

• Sitting in a chair with your eyes closed, imagine calm scenes such as walking on the beach, watching a sunset, laying by a stream in the mountains.

- Sitting in a chair with your eyes closed, focus on parts of your body and tell that part to relax: "My arms are heavy, my hands are warm, my hands are calm, I am relaxed." Do that over and over.
- Practice relaxing thoughts. "I feel relaxed." "I am calm." "I am feeling soothed." "I am feeling cool." "I am feeling quiet." "I am feeling serene."

▶ Breathing relaxation.

- Sit in a comfortable chair, close your eyes and focus on your breathing. Breathe slow and easy and steady, breathing in and out for 5 minutes. Breathe into your stomach and feel your stomach rise and fall. Let the air out completely. As you let the air out, feel yourself sink into the chair.
- After 5 minutes, gradually make your breaths deeper. Then take five deep breaths. Let the air out slowly after each deep breath. Breathe in through your nose, breathe out through your mouth, puckering your lips and blowing out slowly. Always start out breathing slowly and normal and then **do no more than five deep breaths** at a time. Breathe out your tension.

▶ Stretching relaxation.
Stretching lets the tension go out of the muscles and hooks the parts of our body together. **If you have a medical condition, such as a bad back, check with your doctor first before doing stretching exercises.**

- Lay on your back and pull one knee to your chest, stretch the leg back and do the same with the other knee. Pull both knees to your chest. Do these several times.
- Do several sit ups, but do them easy and slow. Feel the muscles stretch.
- Lay on your stomach and push your upper body up by your hands and arms. Do it gently.
- Lay on your side, pull your leg to your chest, then straighten it out and swing it slowly back. Feel the back muscles stretch. Always be gentle and slow. Do this on the other side.
- Now, come up with other stretching exercises. Get a book on stretching.

▶ Muscle relaxation.

- Sit in a chair, close your eyes, put your hands on the chair arms and breathe normally and steadily. Then do deep breathing three times.
- Take about five to ten minutes and go through this muscle exercise with your eyes closed. First, squeeze your eyes closed and then relax the eye muscles. Do this two or three times. Then, squeeze your hands on the chair arms and gradually let the muscles relax. Let go gradually. Do this two times. Squeeze your arm muscles and let them go gradually. Don't squeeze real hard, but tighten them up and then relax them. Go through all of your muscles, your shoulders, your stomach, your thighs, legs and toes. Squeeze gently but tightly.
- At the end of this exercise, with your eyes closed, think of a calm scene. Think relaxing thoughts.

▶ **Active relaxation.**

- Walk 15 minutes a day. Swing your arms for awhile. Put your hands behind your back and walk for awhile reflecting on how good you feel.
- Do as much lifestyle walking each day as you can. Park further away from store entrances so you have to walk to do some exercise.
- Get a set of Shou Xing balls or a soft ball and do hand exercises each day.
- Work out a couple times a week by playing a sport, tennis, go to the gym.

▶ **You can also prepare for stress and life's daily experiences by doing these things.**

- Treat yourself with a massage from time to time.
- Do self-massages such as rubbing your shoulders, your hands, your leg muscles, your feet.
- Sit upright with legs crossed, close your eyes, relax and let your mind go blank.
- Sit in a hot bath or hot tub.
- Develop good sleep patterns.
- Keep your house relaxed with music and pleasant aromas.
- Keep healthy eating habits and a healthy diet.
- Have a quiet time each day and make time for yourself.
- Enjoy nature. Take walks in the woods, a pleasant path, the mountains, in a park. Look at the flowers. Smell the roses.
- Take a vacation.

E. <u>EXERCISE</u>

▶ Using the above relaxation strategies and *Work Sheet 62*, page 214, make a weekly relaxation plan.

▶ For each day write in specific active relaxation strategies you will use.

▶ Each day, plan to do some stretches, mental relaxation and take a walk.

▶ Do an active relaxation only three times a week.

▶ Follow this plan. Change it every so often.

HOMEWORK AND PRESENTING YOUR THERAPY PROJECT

A. Share with your groups the important ideas about relapse prevention.

B. Do your *AOD Weekly Monitoring Chart*.

C. Update your Master Skills Ratings, page 31. Are your ratings getting higher?

Your weekly relaxation plan

WRITE DOWN THE SPECIFIC RELAXATION ACTIVITIES OR STRATEGIES FOR EACH DAY OF THE WEEK.

MONDAY

TUESDAY

WEDNESDAY

THURSDAY

FRIDAY

SATURDAY

SUNDAY

THERAPY PROJECT 5: Preventing Relapse - What is Working Best?

INTRODUCTION

This Therapy Project will focus on what has been working best for you in preventing relapse.

OBJECTIVES FOR THERAPY PROJECT 5

▶ Review *Lessons 8 and 9* in **DWC Level II Education** (page 123-162) and *Sessions 17* and *18* in this workbook (pages 153-174).

▶ Restate your relapse prevention goal. It is preventing relapse into AOD use problems or abstaining from AOD use.

▶ Make a list of those skills that are working best for you in meeting your relapse prevention goal.

THERAPY PROJECT CONTENT AND ACTIVITIES

A. REVIEW THE PARTS OF LESSON 8 OF DWC LEVEL II EDUCATION AND SESSIONS 17 AND 18 OF THIS WORKBOOK THAT DEAL WITH RELAPSE

▶ Relapse begins with high-risk thinking and high-risk situations.

▶ The four triggers for relapse.

▶ The pathways to relapse and the pathways to prevention.

▶ The thinking and action skills to prevent relapse.

B. RESTATE YOUR RELAPSE PREVENTION GOAL IN THE SPACE BELOW.

C. <u>EXERCISE:</u> USING WORK SHEET 63, PAGE 216

▶ List the **thinking skills** you use to prevent relapse.

▶ List the **action skills** you use to prevent relapse.

HOMEWORK AND PRESENTING YOUR THERAPY PROJECT.

A. Share with your groups the important ideas about relapse prevention.

B. Do your *AOD Weekly Monitoring Chart* and update your Master Skills Ratings, page 31.

Thinking and action skills that have been working best for you in preventing relapse.

RELAPSE PREVENTION THINKING SKILLS THAT HAVE WORKED BEST FOR YOU	RELAPSE PREVENTION ACTION SKILLS THAT HAVE WORKED BEST FOR YOU

THERAPY PROJECT 6: Preventing Recidivism - What is Working Best?

INTRODUCTION

This Therapy Project will focus on what has been working best for you in preventing recidivism.

OBJECTIVES OF THERAPY PROJECT 6

▶ Review *Lessons 8 and 9* in **DWC Level II Education** (pages 123-162) and Sessions 17 and 18 (pages 153-174) in this workbook that has to do with recidivism prevention.

▶ Restate your recidivism prevention goal. It can be *preventing legal recidivism* or *zero tolerance-zero risk.*

▶ List those skills that are working best for you in meeting your recidivism prevention goal.

THERAPY PROJECT ACTIVITIES

A. REVIEW THE PARTS OF LESSON 8 OF DWC LEVEL II EDUCATION AND SESSIONS 17 AND 18 OF THIS WORKBOOK THAT DEAL WITH RECIDIVISM

▶ Defining recidivism.

▶ Relapse begins with high-risk thinking and putting yourself in high-risk situations for recidivism.

▶ The pathways to recidivism and recidivism prevention.

▶ The thinking and action skills to prevent recidivism.

B. RESTATE YOUR RECIDIVISM PREVENTION GOAL IN THE SPACE BELOW.

```



```

C. EXERCISE: USING WORK SHEET 64, PAGE 218, LIST THE THINKING AND THE ACTION SKILLS THAT HAVE BEEN WORKING BEST FOR YOU IN PREVENTING RECIDIVISM

▶ List the **thinking skills** you use to prevent recidivism

▶ List the **action skills** you use to prevent recidivism

HOMEWORK AND PRESENTING YOUR THERAPY PROJECT.

A. Share with your groups the important ideas about *relapse prevention.*

B. Do your *AOD Weekly Monitoring Chart* and update your Master Skills Ratings, page 31.

Thinking and action skills that have been working best for you in preventing recidivism.

RECIDIVISM PREVENTION THINKING SKILLS THAT HAVE WORKED BEST FOR YOU	RECIDIVISM PREVENTION ACTION SKILLS THAT HAVE WORKED BEST FOR YOU

THERAPY PROJECT 7: Skills in Time Management and Completing Tasks

INTRODUCTION

Emotional stress and conflict with others can lead to *relapse and recidivism.* One cause of emotional stress and conflict is the pressure to get our work and tasks done or to manage our time. One way we can avoid this stress is to learn to manage our time and the tasks that we have to do.

OBJECTIVES FOR THERAPY PROJECT 7

▶ Learn skills to manage time and completing tasks,

▶ Practice building a weekly schedule to manage time and tasks.

THERAPY PROJECT ACTIVITIES

A. HERE ARE SOME TIME AND TASK MANAGEMENT SKILLS

▶ **Plan ahead.**
   - First, take a few deep breaths and relax.
   - Take a few minutes each evening or at the beginning of each day to plan the day, even if it is your day off from work. Plan it in your head.

▶ **Set your goals.**
   - Plan your outcomes.
   - What do you want to have finished at the end of the day?

▶ **Put what is important first.**
   - This is the most difficult to do.
   - Start with what needs to get done. You will have less stress. We often put the most important or most difficult things last and then go crazy trying to get it done. If the most important thing for you to do today is to buy a birthday present, do it first.

▶ **Timing is the key.**
   - Timing is nine-tenths of success. Start early.
   - Know how much time it will take to do certain jobs or tasks. If you are cooking a meal, figure the time you will need.
   - Add time. We always give ourselves less time than what we think we need to finish a task.

▶ **Time-framing.**

- Give time each day to work on a project or task that is large and has a deadline.

- Waiting to the last minute will make you task-frame. This means working on the task until it is done (or until you drop). That causes stress.

▶ **Task-framing.**

- This may be necessary for the last big push at the end of a task.

- To make task-framing work, you will have to use time-framing for much of the task or project.

- If you task-frame, give yourself enough time.

▶ **Have fun and enjoy.**

- Enjoy what you do and how you approach what you do.

- Give yourself time to enjoy the task or job.

▶ **Look back.**

- Did you meet your goals for the day?

- How was your timing?

- Did you feel stress?

- Did you use the above skills?

- Did you enjoy yourself?

B. <u>EXERCISES</u>

▶ Use the skills above and *Work Sheet 65,* page 221 to practice planning one day.

▶ Plan next week using the *Time-Task Decision Window* in *Work Sheet 66,* page 221. Follow the instructions.

HOMEWORK AND PRESENTING YOUR THERAPY PROJECT

A. Share with your groups the important ideas about relapse prevention.

B. Do your AOD Weekly Monitoring Chart.

C. Look at your *Master Assessment Plan.* How are you doing on the problems you are working on? Talk this over with your counselor.

D. Review your Master Skills List on page 31. Are you mastering some better than others? Update your ratings.

Plan your next day off from work. Describe what you plan to do. What are your goals? Did you task-frame or time-frame your activity? Describe the outcome. Did you have fun?

DESCRIBE YOUR ACTIVITY/TASK	YOUR GOAL OR OUTCOME	TIME IN HOURS	TIME FRAME	TASK FRAME	DESCRIBE YOUR OUTCOME/RESULTS

Your task-time decision window for your next working week. In **Frame One,** put what is most important and what you must get done. In **Frame Two,** put what is less important but what you must get done. In **Frame Three,** put what is most important but doesn't have to get done. In **Frame Four,** put what you don't have to get done and is less important.

	MUST GET DONE	DON'T HAVE TO GET DONE
MOST IMPORTANT	Frame One:	Frame Three:
LESS IMPORTANT	Frame Two:	Frame Four:

THERAPY PROJECT 8: Getting Support from Groups and Others

INTRODUCTION

An important strategy for responsible living and change is to *seek support and help* outside of ourselves. This helps us to be more prosocial. During our growing-up years, we were often taught to solve our own problems, to do it on our own, to "not hang our dirty linen in public." But when we are committed to making change, or have ownership of that change, we are secure enough to reach out and seek help and support from other people or groups that are set up to help people from our community. We have done this within our program group and with our program counselor.

There are outside resources to help you keep up the changes you have made. People who seek the help of others who have problems similar to ours give us support in helping us continue to be responsible and to change.

OBJECTIVES OF THERAPY PROJECT 8

▶ Learn about and make a list of different support groups in your community.

▶ Attend at least two or three of these support groups.

THERAPY PROJECT ACTIVITIES

A. TWO KINDS OF COMMUNITY SUPPORT AND SELF-HELP GROUPS

▶ Those that support you directly in the changes you are trying to make and help you to be more prosocial - such as *Alcoholics Anonymous* (AA).

▶ Those that support you indirectly in your efforts to change and help you live a healthy and prosocial - such as a hiking club, health club or spa, church.

B. EXERCISES

▶ Use *Work Sheet 67,* page 223, to explore the different support and self-help groups in your community. Have the list include the above two kinds of support and self-help groups. Call some of these groups; talk with their members. Make notes as to how this group could support or help you. Use the internet for this project.

▶ Attend three meetings or activities of one of the groups on your list.

HOMEWORK AND PRESENTING YOUR THERAPY PROJECT

A. Share this *Therapy Project* with the group you are in.

B. Do your *AOD Weekly Monitoring Chart.* Review your Master Skills List, page 31.

Making a list of community support and self-help groups. Contact friends, use the Yellow Pages, the internet, and any other source to make a list of community support and self-help groups that might be able to support responsible living and the changes you are making. Include groups that support you directly in your relapse and recidivism prevention goals such as AA; and groups that support you indirectly in your relapse and recidivism prevention goals such as a hiking club, church, etc.

WORKSHEET 67

NAME OF SELF-HELP GROUP	PHONE NUMBER	DATE CONTACTED	YOUR REACTIONS AND COMMENTS

THERAPY PROJECT 9: Giving Support - Mentoring and Role Modeling

INTRODUCTION

The changes we make in our lives become more *stable and permanent* when we become *teachers and mentors* of that change. It is only when we own something that we can share it with someone else. When we have full ownership of responsible living and prosocial actions, we feel secure enough to share with other people the joy and power of the changes we have made.

One way to do this is to become an example, a model or sponsor for other people who are starting to make changes in their lives so that they can live free of AOD problems and legal problems such as impaired driving. This is the wisdom of the AA 12th Step, which is to become sponsors or mentors of others in their effort to change. In this session, we will look at ways that you can become a mentor - a guide, or teacher or tutor - for others.

OBJECTIVES OF THERAPY PROJECT 9

▶ Understand the power of being a role model or mentor for others who are working to change.

▶ Begin to take part in partnerships with other persons who are trying to make changes in AOD use and in criminal conduct.

THERAPY PROJECT ACTIVITIES

A. TWO KINDS OF MENTORSHIPS TO ROLE MODEL CHANGE FOR ANOTHER PERSON

1. **Informal mentoring or role modeling:** This means that you do not directly mentor or sponsor another person. It is informal. You present yourself as someone who has changed, who has control of your life with respect to AOD use and who has a prosocial relationship with others in the community. Other people will see this, will identify with you and want to be "like you."

2. **Formal mentoring:** This is when you formally sponsor someone who has now been challenged to change. You become available for supportive contacts and involvement. You must be ready for this and secure in your own change.

B. SIX SIMPLE STEPS IN BECOMING A MENTOR FOR OTHERS WHO ARE MAKING CHANGES

1. **Feel secure** in your own change and in your ownership of that change.

2. **Know your strengths** at this time in your life as to the changes you have made.

3. **Know your weaknesses** and vulnerable areas and keep track of these as you mentor others. If you are vulnerable when in a bar, then you need to keep that in mind when you are sponsoring or mentoring another person.

4. **Find someone who needs support** in the changes they are making. Be available to them. Use all of the skills you have learned in developing a supportive and healthy relationship with that person.

5. **Find your own mentor,** counselor or sponsor that you can get support from as you mentor or sponsor another person.

6. **Go slow** and lend support to only one person to begin with.

C. <u>EXERCISES</u>

▶ Use *Work Sheet 68, page 226,* to list the strengths that you can bring into a mentorship or sponsorship with another person who is being challenged to change.

▶ Use *Work Sheet 69, page 226,* to list your most vulnerable or weak areas. These are areas that you need to watch closely when you are mentoring or sponsoring someone else.

HOMEWORK AND PRESENTING YOUR THERAPY PROJECT

A. Present this **Therapy Project** and activity to your group.

B. Do your *AOD Weekly Monitoring Chart.*

C. Review your *Master Assessment Plan.* How are you doing with the problem areas you chose to work on? Review these with your counselor.

D. Look over your Master Skills List, page 31. Remember, our goal is for you to rate every skill "good" or "very good."

Your strong areas. Make a list of those areas in which you feel the strongest and most permanent that you can bring to mentoring and role modeling.

LIST THE STRENGTHS YOU CAN BRING TO MENTORING AND ROLE MODELING

Your most vulnerable or weakest areas. Make a list of those areas in which you feel most vulnerable or the weakest and which you need to watch as you mentor and role model.

LIST THE WEAK AREAS YOU NEED TO WATCH AS YOU MENTOR

THERAPY PROJECT 10: Sharing Your Futurography

INTRODUCTION

In your **DWC Therapy** program, you wrote your *autobiography*, which included how you would like your future story to be. We will call this your futurography. The purpose of this therapy project is to write your futurography in more detail.

OBJECTIVES OF THERAPY PROJECT 10

▶ Making future plans.

▶ Stating the kind of person you would like to be.

▶ Thinking about what skills you will need in the future.

▶ Write your futurography.

THERAPY PROJECT ACTIVITIES

A. RE-READ YOUR AUTOBIOGRAPHY AND ANSWER THESE QUESTIONS

▶ Did you leave out some important events? If so, add them.

▶ How will the skills you have learned help you avoid some of the problems you have had in your life?

B. RE-READ YOUR FUTUROGRAPHY PART OF YOUR AUTOBIOGRAPHY AND ANSWER THESE QUESTIONS

▶ Did you leave out some important plans or goals?

▶ Did you describe accurately the way you want to be in the future?

C. WRITE WHAT YOU WANT YOUR FUTURE TO BE

▶ Your future plans and goals.

▶ The kind of person you want to be in the future.

▶ The skills you will use in the future to:

  • be in control of your thinking and actions;

  • have healthy relationships with others; and

  • be prosocial and responsible to your community.

▶ Share your futurography with your group. Ask your group to give you feedback on what you shared.

ALCOHOL AND OTHER DRUGS WEEKLY MONITORING CHART

In column one, put the month and day of your therapy session. Then, for the the week between that session and the next session, put in column two the number of times you thought about drinking or using drugs. In column three, put the number of times you were in a situation where alcohol or other drugs were being used. In column four, put the number of times you used alcohol or drugs. In column five, put the number of times you thought about driving if you drank and in column six whether you drank and drove.

DATE	NUMBER OF TIMES THOUGHT ABOUT DRINKING OR USING DRUGS	NUMBER OF TIMES IN SITUATION WHERE THERE WAS DRINKING OR DRUG USE	NUMBER OF TIMES DRANK OR USED OTHER DRUGS	IF DRANK, NUMBER OF TIMES THOUGHT ABOUT DRIVING	IF DRANK, NUMBER OF TIMES DROVE WHEN DRINKING

ALCOHOL AND OTHER DRUGS WEEKLY MONITORING CHART

In column one, put the month and day of your therapy session. Then, for the the week between that session and the next session, put in column two the number of times you thought about drinking or using drugs. In column three, put the number of times you used alcohol or drugs. In column four, put the number of times you thought about driving if you drank and in column five whether you drank and drove.

DATE	NUMBER OF TIMES THOUGHT ABOUT DRINKING OR USING DRUGS	NUMBER OF TIMES DRANK OR USED OTHER DRUGS	IF DRANK, NUMBER OF TIMES THOUGHT ABOUT DRIVING	IF DRANK, NUMBER OF TIMES DROVE WHEN DRINKING

DRIVING WITH CARE - DWC
CLIENT PROGRESS REPORT - CPR

Name: _____ Agency: _____ Date: _____

Your Program(s): ☐ Level I Education ☐ Level II Education ☐ Level II Therapy

You are asked to answer the following questions as to your involvement in this Program. This is your personal report to your judicial supervisor and the community.

		NO NOT AT ALL	YES SOMEWHAT	YES DEFINITELY
1.	I have paid attention and listened in class.	a	b	c
2.	I took part in group discussions.	a	b	c
3.	I had a positive attitude during DWC.	a	b	c
4.	I was honest and open about my DWI history.	a	b	c
5.	I understand the problems that I have had with the use of alcohol or other drugs.	a	b	c
6.	I understand the seriousness of my past impaired driving behavior and conduct.	a	b	c
7.	I have a good understanding of my alcohol or other drug use patterns.	a	b	c
8.	I have a better understanding of how I can prevent being involved in impaired driving.	a	b	c
9.	I have a relapse prevention plan.	a	b	c
11.	I have a recidivism prevention plan.	a	b	c
12.	I understand how my thinking can lead to DWI behavior.	a	b	c
13.	I will work hard to not let alcohol or other drugs cause me problems in the future.	a	b	c
14.	I agree to never drive with a BAC above the legal limits (.05 if over 21 and .02 if under age 21) or when under the influence of drugs other than alcohol.	a	b	c

The DWC program helped me to...		NO NOT AT ALL	YES SOMEWHAT	YES FOR SURE
15.	Understand the laws related to impaired driving in my state.	a	b	c
16.	Understand the process of recidivism into impaired driving.	a	b	c
17.	Understand the process of relapse.	a	b	c
18.	Understand how thinking leads to actions.	a	b	c
19.	Understand the patterns and styles of AOD use.	a	b	c

The DWC program helped me to...

		NO NOT AT ALL	YES SOMEWHAT	YES FOR SURE
20.	Understand the facts and ideas about alcohol and other drugs.	a	b	c
21.	Understand the kind of problems that can come from alcohol or other drug use.	a	b	c

		NO	SOMETIMES	MOST THE TIME	ALL OF THE TIME
22.	I read the lessons before going to class.	a	b	c	d
23.	I did the work sheets in my workbook.	a	b	c	d
24.	I did the homework exercises.	a	b	c	d
25.	I found it easy to stay away from the use of alcohol during the program.	a	b	c	d
26.	I found it easy to stay away from the use of other drugs during the program.	a	b	c	d
27.	I found it easy to avoid drinking and driving during the program.	a	b	c	d

Now, please answer the following questions.

		NO NOT AT ALL	YES SOMEWHAT	YES FOR SURE
28.	The DWC staff or counselors were helpful.	a	b	c
29.	The DWC workbook was helpful.	a	b	c
30.	Overall, the DWC program was helpful.	a	b	c
31.	I would recommend the DWC program to others.	a	b	c

32. The progress you have made in preventing involvement in impaired driving.

☐ a. I have made no progress.
☐ b. I have made some progress.
☐ c. I have made quite a bit of progress.
☐ d. I have made a lot of progress.

33. At this time, do you think that you have a problem with alcohol or other drug use?

☐ a. No, not at this time.
☐ b. I might have a problem, but I am not sure.
☐ c. I still have a problem.
☐ d. I still have a serious problem with alcohol use.

34. What additional services or help do you think that you need?

☐ a. Group counseling.
☐ b. Individual counseling.
☐ c. Family counseling.
☐ d. Alcohol and drug education.
☐ e. Relapse/recidivism prevention.
☐ f. Support group.
☐ g. Antabuse.
☐ h. Ignition interlock.
☐ i. Other services.

35. What has been the most helpful about DWC?

I understand that this Client Progress Report will be sent to my probation officer or judicial supervisor.

DRIVING WITH CARE - DWC
CLIENT PROGRESS REPORT - CPR

Name: _____ Agency: _____ Date: _____

Your Program(s): ☐ Level I Education ☐ Level II Education ☐ Level II Therapy

You are asked to answer the following questions as to your involvement in this Program. This is your personal report to your judicial supervisor and the community.

		NO NOT AT ALL	YES SOMEWHAT	YES DEFINITELY
1.	I have paid attention and listened in class.	a	b	c
2.	I took part in group discussions.	a	b	c
3.	I had a positive attitude during DWC.	a	b	c
4.	I was honest and open about my DWI history.	a	b	c
5.	I understand the problems that I have had with the use of alcohol or other drugs.	a	b	c
6.	I understand the seriousness of my past impaired driving behavior and conduct.	a	b	c
7.	I have a good understanding of my alcohol or other drug use patterns.	a	b	c
8.	I have a better understanding of how I can prevent being involved in impaired driving.	a	b	c
9.	I have a relapse prevention plan.	a	b	c
11.	I have a recidivism prevention plan.	a	b	c
12.	I understand how my thinking can lead to DWI behavior.	a	b	c
13.	I will work hard to not let alcohol or other drugs cause me problems in the future.	a	b	c
14.	I agree to never drive with a BAC above the legal limits (.05 if over 21 and .02 if under age 21) or when under the influence of drugs other than alcohol.	a	b	c

The DWC program helped me to...	NO NOT AT ALL	YES SOMEWHAT	YES FOR SURE
15. Understand the laws related to impaired driving in my state.	a	b	c
16. Understand the process of recidivism into impaired driving.	a	b	c
17. Understand the process of relapse.	a	b	c
18. Understand how thinking leads to actions.	a	b	c
19. Understand the patterns and styles of AOD use.	a	b	c

The DWC program helped me to...		NO NOT AT ALL	YES SOMEWHAT	YES FOR SURE
20.	Understand the facts and ideas about alcohol and other drugs.	a	b	c
21.	Understand the kind of problems that can come from alcohol or other drug use.	a	b	c

		NO	SOMETIMES	MOST THE TIME	ALL OF THE TIME
22.	I read the lessons before going to class.	a	b	c	d
23.	I did the work sheets in my workbook.	a	b	c	d
24.	I did the homework exercises.	a	b	c	d
25.	I found it easy to stay away from the use of alcohol during the program.	a	b	c	d
26.	I found it easy to stay away from the use of other drugs during the program.	a	b	c	d
27.	I found it easy to avoid drinking and driving during the program.	a	b	c	d

Now, please answer the following questions.		NO NOT AT ALL	YES SOMEWHAT	YES FOR SURE
28.	The DWC staff or counselors were helpful.	a	b	c
29.	The DWC workbook was helpful.	a	b	c
30.	Overall, the DWC program was helpful.	a	b	c
31.	I would recommend the DWC program to others.	a	b	c

32. The progress you have made in preventing involvement in impaired driving.

    ❑ a. I have made no progress.
    ❑ b. I have made some progress.
    ❑ c. I have made quite a bit of progress.
    ❑ d. I have made a lot of progress.

33. At this time, do you think that you have a problem with alcohol or other drug use?

    ❑ a. No, not at this time.
    ❑ b. I might have a problem, but I am not sure.
    ❑ c. I still have a problem.
    ❑ d. I still have a serious problem with alcohol use.

34. What additional services or help do you think that you need?

    ❑ a.   Group counseling.   ❑ f. Support group.
    ❑ b.   Individual counseling.   ❑ g. Antabuse.
    ❑ c.   Family counseling.   ❑ h. Ignition interlock.
    ❑ d.   Alcohol and drug education.   ❑ i. Other services.
    ❑ e.   Relapse/recidivism prevention.

35. What has been the most helpful about DWC?

I understand that this Client Progress Report will be sent to my probation officer or judicial supervisor.